T0065500

There Is
Now No
Condemnation

21st Century Christian Counseling Without Compromise

BERYL I. COWTHRAN, PH.D.

WESTBOW
PRESS®
A DIVISION OF THOMAS NELSON
& ZONDERVAN

WestBow Press books may be ordered through booksellers or by contacting:

WestBow Press
A Division of Thomas Nelson & Zondervan
1663 Liberty Drive
Bloomington, IN 47403
www.westbowpress.com
844-714-3454

Scripture taken from the King James Version® and New King James Version® Copyright © 1982 by Thomas Nelson. Used by permission. All rights reserved.

ISBN: 978-1-6642-3022-4 (sc)
ISBN: 978-1-6642-3021-7 (e)

Print information available on the last page.

WestBow Press rev. date: 5/28/2021

CONTENTS

PART 3: COMPASSIONATE COUNSELING WITHOUT CONDEMNATION IN THE 21ST CENTURY

DEDICATION

To the Father, Son, and Holy Spirit for your
eternal love and amazing grace.

To my father, Reverend Dr. Athan Cowthran, Jr., who taught
me to love God by loving, serving, and caring for others. To
my niece, Madison Alise Critton, who never met my father,
but I hope she will see God's manifested work in me and
continue the family legacy of loving and serving God and His
people. To my maternal grandparents, Deacon M.T. Lee for
your unwavering, uncompromising, steadfast faith and Mrs.
Gennie V. Jones Lee who embodied beautiful, bold humility.
And to my paternal grandparents, Reverend Athan Cowthran,
Sr., for your years of unyielding preaching and Mrs. Scharlotte
Roberson Cowthran, for setting the example to finish.

ACKNOWLEDGMENT

I am grateful to my mother, Betty Jane Lee Cowthran, for her nurturing support and fervent prayers. I cannot remember a time in my life that Mother has not been cheering and encouraging me. Her support has been invaluable during this project as with anything else. She is such a nurturer to leaders in the body of Christ, encourager to those struggling with life's challenges, and an extender of God's love and grace.

Aunt Sally, thank you for your gentle push and believing prayers. Your obedience to the prophetic voice of God has landed me in His Will.

How can I say thanks to my "front row," who are always cheering, coaching, and challenging me simply to be me? Elle Aay, thank you for sharing your struggles to assist me with developing my strengths.

Pastor Brian Scott, I am blessed to be covered in ministry by you. Your wisdom and consistent counsel are unparalleled gifts. Thank you for encouraging me to see the blessing in discomfort and for introducing me to "thriving" ministry.

Dr. Mary Rounds, your editorial contribution and act of love will never be forgotten. Mr. Billy Williams thank you for reviewing the subject matter with grace.

PREFACE

You have heard it said that there are two sides to every story. My Aunt Dorothy would always say, "There are two sides to every story and even a third one sometimes." My Big Mama would warn me to take the side of God even when it disagreed with me. As I sat watching the news, I realized that the world is a very different place than what I had remembered growing up. Things have taken an abrupt about face. The evolution of things seems to be happening at the speed of light. As I allowed the reflections of the day to roll around in my head, stirred by the residual pain of my own personal issues, seasoned with the saltiness of bitter people, baked by the heated political climate, I realized that I could no longer remain quiet or casual regarding certain issues. I am not sure if what I refer to as "issues" are indeed issues for those who make certain choices. I do know for sure that as a pastor in the 21st century it is unacceptable for me to wait until a problem or issue arises before I decide to address it or look for its answer. Our world is full of issues, debates, problems, discriminations, and dilemmas. How can I have a Father who knows all things and is the God of all grace, and yet, act as if these things are not my problem? How can I look the other way, leaving the door closed on these issues?

There is another saying that you may have heard, "Ignorance of the law is not an excuse." The Word of God tells us in 2 Timothy 2:15–17 (KJV),

"Study to shew thyself approved unto God, a workman that needeth not to be ashamed, rightly dividing the word of truth. But shun profane and vain babblings: for they will increase unto more ungodliness. And their word will eat as doth a canker: of whom is Hymenaeus and Philetus;"

As a Christian, ignorance of the Word of God is not an excuse. Joshua 1:8 urges that Christians meditate on the law of the Lord both day and night. We are to study the Word. As I continued sitting up in bed trying to focus between the news and the thoughts which had now dominated my convictions, I decided to explore just a bit further. I decided to take Big Mama's advice and by doing so, I decided to take the side of God. As a pastor, teacher, and Christian counselor, I surmised it was a great idea to explore what Aunt Dorothy had often said to me. Again, she warned that there were two sides to every story and often a third. That's when I decided to take a look at relativism, the ambiguity underlying our moral truths. Having grown up in the church, I have seen so many people have "issues" yet serve and love God. How can other people in church who, by the way, have their own faults and issues state so freely that other people are going to hell? How could they judge and not extend grace? Where is the compassion?

While reflecting, I realized that one of the goals in counseling for me is to guide counselees to the *one* answer *who* I know never fails, Jesus. I also realized that I have never had a cookie-cutter solution for how to get to the answers needed for counselees. Although the path to successful counseling is *different* for many, the right answer is clearly in the *same* place. The right answer has to be a righteous answer. To help people get there, we, the church, must understand the ministry of grace. I began to wonder how I can address certain topics with counselees without making them feel uncomfortable or risking feeling uncomfortable myself. I have never wanted to hurt anyone's feelings. What if my confrontation of sin in the counselee's life causes hurt feelings? Reverend Brian Scott says that our assignment isn't a choice; it's a challenge! As a Christian, it is my challenge to help others. I decided *not* to ignore the problems that I had no understanding of. Proverbs 4:5–9 (KJV) says,

> "Get wisdom, get understanding: forget it not; neither decline from the words of my mouth. Forsake her not, and she shall preserve thee: love her, and she shall keep thee. Wisdom is the principal thing; therefore get wisdom: and with all thy getting get understanding. Exalt her, and she shall promote thee: she shall bring thee to honour, when thou dost embrace her. She shall give to thine head an ornament of grace: a crown of glory shall she deliver to thee."

Grammatically, there is an understood "you" as the subject. That means, the reader of Proverbs 4:5–9 is the "you" who is supposed to get wisdom, understanding, and exalt her (wisdom). Hence, I decided to write this book for the counselor and the counselee. Although it is written *for* them, it is also written to everyone regarding 21st century hot topics.

In counseling, it should be our goal to come together for the highest good of the counselee. In the church, we should come together for the highest good of mankind, especially those of the household of faith. This book has been written to address the space in between. By no means is a this a comprehensive guide to counseling. However, it is a place where the two can work from the marginalization of personal perspectives to meet at *uncommon, common* ground of God's Holy Word.

INTRODUCTION

The *gift* of Christian counseling is in high demand. The scriptures are important to the vitality of Christian living. The living Word of God is the guiding force for living a purpose filled life. An honest review of the latest news and current events supports the fact that our world needs an on-going infusion of biblical truths. The purpose of this book is to further support the claim for Christian counseling in contemporary times. While the world keeps scratching its head and succumbing to many of the societal pressures, the church can continue to provide irrefutable, life-changing answers from the Word of God.

At the time of this writing, the entire world is experiencing a pandemic. COVID-19 has changed headlines, conversations, graduations, weddings, vacation plans, church services, standards of operations, policies, and procedures for just about everyone globally. No matter how we are characterized or choose to be characterized, the pandemic has become a common denominator for us all. As the world deals with the fragmented pieces left behind from the alarming amount of death, job loss, and economic disparity, we are found trying to make a whole new life with the fractions we have left. In the midst of everything, systemic racism continues to take its bow front and center on the stage of American soil. Although, the pandemic serves as the common denominator globally, things still do not add up. The numerator is yet unbalanced as many groups fight, kill, and steal to be on top. The imbalance has resulted in protests in all fifty states of the union and numerous other countries. Police brutality against black people in America and other people of color (inclusive of people who are not considered white, Caucasian, or of European descent in some cases), gender inequality, homelessness among transgender teens, healthcare disparities, equal pay, and much more compete for prioritization on the list of complaints and protests. Both preachers and politicians have taken to the streets to march alongside those who are simply exhausted with the age-old systems of inequality.

A blind person sees that these are not issues at which we can only take a glance. The depths of pain and the cries and groans of many are no longer something that we can place on mute, push pause, walk away from, and/or look in the other direction. Television, social media, and radio stations across the world have all been on the same frequency. Can the church and our government solve the problems we have been facing for centuries? What does separation of church and state mean when it involves the same people enduring the same pain? As individuals, including parishioners, preachers, and politicians, took to the frontlines in protest of discrimination and disparities, many were still burying their fallen from COVID-19. Preachers and politicians are responding to the same problems, but often, with different agendas. Categories, subcategories, committees, and subcommittees have only served to create a greater divergence between groups of people. The resulting hole leaves us anything but whole and is often packed with occupants such as hatred, discrimination, tension, and hostility; thereby, leaving little room for love to abide.

With increasing cries of those who wish to be heard and acknowledged, we witness increasing groups, cells, silos, and other divisions. Do we have to be divided to be diverse? Can we celebrate diversity without division? Often, we have the right agenda with the wrong action. Our collective goal should be reaching equality for all humanity. Without equality, an equitable balance cannot be attained. Much needed conversations have been dominated by unwanted controversy regarding race, gender, sexual orientation, economic and health disparities. Holding these conversations "in one nation under God" can be quite controversial. Religion is not always relational, and denominations often do not share a common denominator even when it comes to "God." One nation, America, with a diverse group of individuals who make up and contribute to it, often looks like many nations tucked in their own corners. *Was* this the intent of the nation's forefathers? Furthermore, *is* this the intent of the heavenly Father? Is there really any religious "freedom" in America? Moral and cultural relativism are only the tip of the iceberg. How each individual manages his or her perspective relative to humanity may be determined by the cultural, economic, sexual, racial lens through which one sees. These are only a few of many lenses. How terrible would it be to visit an ophthalmologist needing corrective vision-ware only to be given the prescription fit for the ophthalmologist? This is often what happens when leaders are not compassionate and empathetic. Hence, politicians, parents, public servants, chief executives, managers, team leaders, supervisors, and all leaders must be conscientious regarding the messages and visuals given to those who follow and are left influenced. Often, professed Christians fill these positions. Is there a place for moral responsibility in the workplace? Does that responsibility have to be graded or viewed by means of some assessment tool for accountability's sake?

Although this book is written *to* Christian counselors and counselees, it is written *for* every person to read. As you are reading along here, you see intentional use of words like "self" and "whosoever". These are throughout the manuscript for relational purposes with the reader and the Bible. I also endeavor in this work to address numerous questions that we all have regarding our current state of affairs, whether it be economically, spiritually, emotionally, sexually, and even artificially (I will explain later). The sum total of who we are is not given to one of these things, but more importantly is where we are plotted holistically. To have this discussion, I have written this book in three parts. Admittedly, Part I is the foundational work for which the remaining parts have been written. It may be the toughest part and seemingly most irrelevant upon first glance. I promise you that the necessity of the first six chapters will become apparent as you continue the thought-provoking journey. As you extend grace to me in these chapters, you will build a perspective before diving into the last six chapters. Part II is transitional and designed to prepare readers for asking and addressing questions. In Part III, I deal with the many "shhh" or hushed issues. How will the church address and/or approach these issues? Our tendency, as a whole, is to focus on the flood while forgetting about the dripping faucets in other rooms. We know that we have twisted the knobs to the off position; but behind, the wall is often forgotten pool of spilling water which only gets our attention when the mold and mildew began to cry and yell in protest. Let's open the door on these issues and take a look at the leak.

PART I

RELATIVISM AND CHRISTIAN COUNSELING

CHAPTER 1

THE DILEMMA AND THE DESIRE: 21ST CENTURY COUNSELING

The Dilemma of 21st Century Counseling

Is the scripture sufficient for counseling? Are Christian counselors compassionate? Do Christian counselors find themselves compromising the scripture to "compensate" and "accommodate" counselees? These are only a few of the points that Christian counselors, pastors, preachers, teachers, evangelists, and all Christians –period– must ponder. With changes in policies and legislation, could the borders within which Christian counselors work be closing in, and in some cases even collapsing? It seems that in times past, counselors have been somewhat protected by a shield of laws, legislature, and policies. With the ever-changing political climate in America, counselors are working with more clients who will choose to disclose more. With the push for new laws and the redefining of protective classes in America, counselors engage in dialogue that once upon a time remained buried deep below the surface. Counselors must recognize that they will not have that shield of "protection" as they counsel a new "protected" class of citizens.

Counselors must be cognizant of the potential pitfalls and temptations associated with moral relativism. When considering the desired goal of counseling, counselors, as faith proponents, must be able to distinguish between faith at work versus idealistic distortion, which clouds reality for the counselee. How does the counselor balance the need to be empathetic –yet uncompromising– or to have faith for a seemingly impossible outcome without crossing the line into idealistic distortion? Counselors must be able to answer the *call* to fulfill the ministry assignment of counseling while being able to *answer* some of the toughest and most controversial questions with which human beings have grappled.

The Desire for 21st Century Counseling

The desire of Christian counselors lies within helping counselees to discover and apply biblical solutions. Are counselors ready to present the gospel uncompromisingly balanced with presenting the love of Christ compassionately? Christians must be conscientious not to allow *political* correctness to be the guiding force for the depth of *Christian* counseling given. The guidance of the Holy Spirit and reliance thereupon are so vitally important. Consequently, the Holy Bible should be referred to as *the source* for counseling, and all other material should be considered as *resources*.

Counselors should aim to meet the need of counselees by applying an age-old Word to both old and contemporary problems and issues. The church often struggles with remaining relevant in a contemporary, ever-evolving world. Often, this struggle results in *compromise*. Christians, overall, must not shy away from the address of existent and increasingly prevalent difficult topics which are becoming common among us. Instead, one must willingly research scripture for an authentic meaning. Why an authentic meaning? Too often, scripture is dressed and adorned in an interpretation suitable for one's personal pleasure or it is stripped for the same reason. The search for the authentic meaning of scripture serves as a preventative approach against erroneous counsel, which can easily be based on opinion or moral relativism. The temptation to render opinion or to be swayed morally based on culture or personal desires is ever pressing when there is a lack of substantiated evidence of past counseling outcomes which may be similar to the counselees "current" experience. Counselors must build upon past experiences and present the Holy Bible as truth, and not as an anthological compilation of fiction. Past experiences, whether victorious or unsuccessful, can provide the most valuable experience forward for others in need of godly solutions. While substantiated and statistical data are great tools to have, Christian counselors must not allow this data to preclude faith. Faith is important *now* for the *future*. It is the necessary piece of Christian counseling which keeps the counselor and counselee working forward for the best outcome. Again, the counselor's dependency on the Holy Spirit is paramount. Any Christian who gives counsel of any kind should direct the counselee to have faith that is consistent with the teachings of God. Often the reality of the counselee is so daunting that he or she may choose faith as some idealistic escape from their norm. If this ideal does not agree with the Word of God, the counselee can become subjected to idealistic distortion, which we will talk about in Chapter 2.

As Christian counselors practice love and respond in love according to John 3:17, better outcomes will be more frequent. While protected classes and other subject matters are being redefined, the definition of love according to God's will needs no redefining. It needs to be both *re-presented* and represented. The Truth, the Word of God, should be spoken in love. The question arises, "Who's truth is it?" It is important to know what both the counselor and counselee consider as truth. Is it relative to God or to the person who is speaking at the time? Christians should speak Truth according to God's Holy Word and not merely to fit their personal desires or the desires of those in need of counsel. Bible-based counseling in the 21st century will not only be possible but will be successful when two main pieces are prioritized: truth and love. When the profession of one's faith in God is held on to without wavering, the door of compromise will remain closed. As Christians, we should endeavor to maintain our own relationship with God if we desire to lead the counselee in the direction of positive outcomes. Jeremiah 31:3 (NKJV) says, "The Lord has appeared of old to me, saying: 'Yes, I have loved you with an everlasting love; Therefore, with lovingkindness have I drawn you.'" If the church of God is going to continue surviving and thriving in the 21st century, counselors need to be intentional about ensuring that the love of God is activated in the life of the counselee. This often requires for him or her to be saved. Rick Warren said,

> "Our culture has accepted two huge lies. The first is that if you disagree with someone's lifestyle, you must fear or hate them. The second is that to love someone means you agree with everything they believe or do. Both are nonsense. You don't have to compromise convictions to be compassionate."[1]

How well does Warren's last statement summarize what should be our resolve? How can we judge others and expect to lead them to salvation?

I have spent time freely speaking with people from the LGBTQ community, science community, women and men who have experienced abortion, and the Christian community. The Christian community is mentioned last because there is a great tendency to place ourselves both first and final in an argument. What happens to our belief system after we have listened to others? Will it be proven to be able to withstand challenging seasons? Our belief system does not have to be altered in order for us to have compassion for others. Perhaps, it is *our* heart that needs a bit of work. Cardiologists would contend that open heart surgery does not change the name and the identity of the person who undergoes the procedure. We do not have to compromise who we are as Christians to have a change of heart and compassion for others. As Christians, we must allow God to circumcise our own hearts and be willing to bypass pride, self-righteousness, and the urge to judge so that uncompromising love will reign.

We also must learn that conformity is not compassion. Our goal should be to strive toward doing good. Such examples must be set for counselees. James 4:17 teaches that the one who knows the good they ought to do and does not do it, it is sin for him or her.[2] Matthew 5:16 commands us to allow our light to "so" shine before men, that they may see our good works, and glorify our Father which is in heaven.[3] What is good? The answer may be dependent upon whether one looks through the prism of moral relativism, through the tunnel of one's own ideology, or through the eyes of absolutism.

CHAPTER 2

MORAL RELATIVISM

Who or what establishes what is moral or immoral? Plausible or not, it seems that most people consult the internet for everything from do-it-yourself projects to diagnosing physical ailments. Religious topics and morality are not excluded from the search. The Internet Encyclopedia of Philosophy defines morality as the view that moral judgments are true or false only relative to some particular standpoint (for instance, that of a culture or a historical period and that no standpoint is uniquely privileged over all others.)[4] Could the implication of this definition be that moral compliance is judged at the level of human beings and not by the supreme God? Moral relativism not only suggests that no standpoint is uniquely privileged over all the others, but it also implies that there is no universal set of morals. A search of the definition of both morals and morality yields varying, yet similar definitions. The definitions contain subjective terminology such as "wrong," "right," "good," "bad," and others. The prevailing issue with this subjective terminology is that it results in ambiguity and leaves room for personal and cultural interpretation. Lucy Ann Moll suggests that moral relativism is old news dating back to the Garden of Eden, where the smooth-talking serpent seduced Adam and Eve.[5] In Chapter 8 of the gospel of Mark, we are introduced to Jesus as He enters Bethsaida. Verses 22–26 record that a blind man was brought to Him for healing.[6]

Deciding to take the man out of the town, Jesus spat on his eyes and posed a question. After putting His hands on the man, the all-wise, all-knowing Jesus asked him if he saw anything. What follows is very interesting and has been interpreted several ways. The man answers, "I see men as trees, walking."[7] Jesus places His hands on the man a second time and he sees every man clearly from that point.[8]

Among theologians and Christian commentators alone, there are several interpretations of the same text. Are they all wrong or, all right? Let's consider a few of them. Could the progressive healing of the man have been because he struggled with doubt? Surely, the healing could have taken place immediately. Could the progressive healing of the man be a picture of the disciples' slow, but progressive spiritual comprehension as suggested in the King James Study Bible?[9] Was this a lesson regarding perception being that he saw men as trees walking? Was it an exercise in believing God when things do not fully materialize the first time? Is there an appreciation in the text for friends who have faith enough to bring their friend to God? Considering that the scripture says that they brought their friend to Jesus and Jesus took him out of town, should we learn from them how to let go and let God? Could the implication be that our walk with the Lord is a gradual process? Matthew Henry suggests that the blind man, himself, did not display the earnestness that other blind men had demonstrated in expectation of receiving healing.[10] Is this really the case or is this what Mr. Henry needed to receive from the text personally? There are no "clear-cut" answers to the aforementioned; however, the work of the Holy Spirit is always precise! Christian counselors need not only the assistance of the Holy Spirit, but also His guidance. For me, presently, I view this text through a different lens. As stated in the introduction, Christians are often given to cells, silos, groups, committees, and categories. As I pen this narrative, the world has been in practice of peaceful protests. Considering recent events, I believe that it is our Christian responsibility to look within ourselves and evaluate the presence of racism, biases, discrimination, subjectivities, proclivities, and other evils that have the unhealthy potential for clouding our vision. Perhaps when we look within, we will find that we, too, need another touch. For me, it is a question of how we see humanity. The man in the text did not see humanity as it was created. Instead, he saw men as trees, walking. When Jesus is asking the questions, it is very difficult to lie about what we see. However, when we allow ourselves to ask these questions apart from Him, we leave the door open to false perspectives and willful blindness in areas which need correction.

This particular text demonstrates the importance of both proper interpretation and life application. While the Christian counselor is highly encouraged to include scripture as part of any counseling material and session, he or she must use it wisely and responsibly. Scripture should never be used to fit the desires of the counselor nor the counselee. Instead, it is used to guide and meet the need of the counselor in providing the tools to help the counselee navigate life. When helping someone in need, Christian counselors are to beware of sharing cookie-cutter solutions. Each individual presenting with a need for counseling for the first time should be treated as a unique experience. When performed, a root cause analysis may reveal something very different and deeper than what presents at the surface. Performing an analysis is a great practice, which should be used consistently throughout counseling. This allows for more timely, appropriate, and contextual application of the Word.

Is Relativism Reliable?

Some would contend that moral value is only applicable within the cultural, social, personal, and/or historical boundaries for which the moral is practiced. Moral relativism is subdivided into at least three positions: descriptive, meta-ethical, and normative. **Descriptive moral relativism** states or describes the way things are or as they are observed based on cultural and social diverseness.[11] **Meta-ethical**

moral relativism is more subjective and self-relating.[12] This position explores how "I" see things and proposes that there is no universal guide for morals. **Normative moral relativism** objectively suggests that everyone has an opinion which should be tolerated because no universal standard is available.[13] The reliability of relativism is most often tested within the window of these three positions.

Descriptive Moral Relativism

The Christian counselor who is committed to successful outcomes will witness few if the main goal of counseling is simply to identify the problem(s) within the parameters of a particular cultural and/or social setting. Descriptive moral relativism considers that there may be varying moral codes based on different cultures and social practices. This position is viewed mainly from the anthropological perspective and does not yield for intentional incorporation of the Holy Spirit's omnispective. The work of the Holy Spirit is paramount in the Christian counseling setting. Christian counsel cannot be effective independent of the Holy Spirit. He guides beyond the surfaces of what is seen and reveals those things which may be seemingly hidden. He even works to lead the way to recovery, reconciliation, and renewal. He opens our eyes to that which is not yet seen. On the contrary, descriptive moral relativists hold that moral values may be based on cultural diversity. Morals as described here are based on the traditions and/or practices of a particular culture or society. The descriptive moral relativist believes that morals are shaped by those traditions and/or practices.

Where does moral responsibility fit in relation to descriptive moral relativism? Subscribing to this particular position can result in a risk for moral irresponsibility and compromised counseling. How so? Well, a thorough counseling session involves gathering some background information regarding familial and demographical details. Often, the information gathered from the counselee is useful for the root cause analysis in reference to the issue(s) or problem(s). If the counselor discovers a problem relative to cultural bias, tradition, or practice, the counselee may not see it as a problem at all if he or she is a descriptive moral relativist. He or she may identify the problem as a social or cultural norm, something which is widely accepted and widely practiced. Counselors must be knowledgeable of this common pitfall. Just because something is culturally acceptable does not mean that it is biblically soundproof. Gaining successful outcomes will be challenging if the counselor or counselee cannot view a social or cultural norm through the spiritual lens and light of God's Word. Moral responsibility will be scarce and excuses plentiful in a setting where morals are descriptive based on cultural and/or social acceptance. This position in counseling compromises the potential for positive outcomes because what is wrong may be viewed as acceptable or what is right may be viewed as unacceptable within a group. The counselor or counselee who views things through the cultural or social lens risks seeing things as they can be described at a present time rather than as they should be. Let us consider the potential danger of seeing things only as they are *descriptively*. If indeed a practice or tradition justifies what is moral, what justifies the practice or tradition? Deuteronomy 12:29–31 (KJV) says,

> "When the LORD thy God shall cut off the nations from before thee, whither thou goest to possess them, and thou succeedest them, and dwellest in their land; Take heed to thyself that thou be not snared by following them, after that they be destroyed from before thee; and that thou enquire not after their gods, saying, How did these nations serve their gods? even so will I do likewise. Thou shalt not do so unto the LORD thy God: for every abomination to the LORD, which he hateth, have they done unto their gods; for even their sons and their daughters they have burnt in the fire to their gods."

The Lord explicitly warns the children of Israel not to fall prey to the practices of the nations who would be cut off before them. He warns them not to inquire about the gods of those nations and not to offer (the same) sacrifices to Him which had been offered to their gods. He especially noted that they had practiced burning their sons and daughters as a sacrificial offering. Subscribers to descriptive moral relativism would contend against God. If moral value is based on the cultural and social acceptance of traditions and practices, then it would be morally permissive to kill sons and daughters against the will of God. Someone agreeing with this position would not question the moral relevance of this practice. That person would believe that it is simply the cultural practice of that group. Because something is a culturally embedded practice and traditionally executed does not mean it is right to do. Hence the practice does not result in reliability. In contemporary times, society has made some people feel it is okay to abort healthy babies. How do counselors prepare for similar situations in the counseling session? They must not only be biblically sound, but also well informed on cultural diversity and biases. Only knowing one's own perspective and not that of others leads to inadequate counseling. It is important that Christians be open to listen to the concerns and perspectives of others before offering solutions.

Cultural and social evolutions occur over time often resulting in a biological, physical, environmental, economic, and/or ecological shift. These evolutions may demand a shift in behavior which could result in the shift of moral values as well. Could a community plagued by a declining economy argue that it's okay to steal based on the description of its shifting culture? How would shifts in a culture establish new norms without disrupting moral value? Consider Darwin's Theories of Evolution and Natural Selection along with the Big Bang Theory. These are based upon an anthropological description. They suggest that human adaptation took place progressively. There is an implication that in order to adjust and adapt to evolutionary changes, some practices and methodologies would also be subject to change; thereby, shifting and reshaping beliefs, practices, and moral behaviors. Christians and counselors, hoping to contribute toward the good of society and build the kingdom, should consider changes in current events and how they have the potential to shift and reshape moral values both directly and indirectly. Charles Darwin said that it is not the strongest or the most intelligent of the species that survive, but the one most adaptive to change.[14] Descriptive moral relativists may be *responsive* yet not *responsible*. They may do what it takes to survive based on the current cultural and social acceptances; however, they will ascribe moral value based on certain exceptions. Let's consider looting and rioting. While these occurrences, burning down buildings, destroying property, and stealing, are illegal, some individuals may engage in these activities when there has been a shift in the political climate or presence of social injustice. As so many African Americans have experienced police brutality resulting in the unnecessary death of many, peaceful protests went awry. The result became the burning of businesses and communities and looting inside many of them. Some people exclaimed in fury and deep pain over the loss of businesses and the ruin of communities. The looting of merchandise was witnessed across America as media outlets filmed real-time. There was another corner of America infuriated that their peaceful protests of police brutality against black lives had gone ignored. Many of them, who would not have engaged in illegal activity, such as arson or theft, on a typical day, were participants during the shift, which followed the death of Mr. George Floyd in Minnesota on Memorial Day 2020. I am not condoning the actions of arson and theft. However, if we look at one side of the coin, we may miss the full value of how it is spent.

Meta-ethical Moral Relativism

The Stanford Encyclopedia of Philosophy defines meta-ethical moral relativism as the position that the truth or falsity of moral judgments, or their justification, is not absolute or universal, but is relative to the traditions, convictions, or practices of a group of persons.[15] This position states that there is no *objectivity* surrounding morals and that everything is *subjective* to the one or the group for which the moral is "about." This argument places the judgment of what is considered right or wrong on the person or group for which the moral decision is about. While descriptive moral relativism settles with things as they are and does not suggest how they should be, meta-ethical relativism looks at how things should be based on the traditions and practices of the person or group of people who share a common culture. Descriptive moral relativism simply acknowledges that some people disagree about what is moral. Meta-ethical relativism holds that nobody is right or wrong and that moral correctness is based within "self." "Self" represents where the moral originates or comes from. This held view leads to ethical subjectivism. Mark M. H. Tan states that ethical subjectivism suggests that ethics is a matter of subjective preferences.[16] Plainly, ethical subjectivity is based on the individual or "self." Like all other positions of moral relativism, this view contends that there is no universal moral code. If "self" is the moral standard, where is the standard? Is there really a standard if one is left to himself or herself to decide what is right or wrong? If individual cultures and persons are able to determine what is moral behavior, in some cases it may result in lawlessness. 1 John 3:4 tells us that whoever commits a sin is guilty of transgressing the law and that sin is transgression of the law.[17] Christians offering counsel, especially Christian counselors, must be attentive to this. Of course, the goal of Christian counseling is not necessarily that the counselor and counselee agree on everything. It is permissible for them not to agree on a favorite color, community living, preferences in food, hair color, and so on. However, it is important for the counselor not to compromise his or her faith in God nor the proper application of scripture to accommodate any beliefs of the counselee that may be in contradiction of the scripture. As with descriptive moral relativism, what happens when what is right for "self" is wrong for someone else or everyone? These dangers of meta-ethical moral relativism are very similar to that of descriptive moral relativism.

However, there is an advantage of meta-ethical moral relativism that can be carefully incorporated into the counseling session. This position can promote moral responsibility by encouraging the counselee to consider his or her own moral behavior. Wow! Just think if all humanity considered his or her own moral behavior! The disadvantage is that the behavior will most often be tried against the backdrop of one's own culture or thoughts. If that backdrop has a crack in it, the wrong behaviors may be permissible. In Act 1, Scene III of William Shakespeare's *Hamlet,* Polonius says,

> This above all: to thine own self be true
> And it must follow, as the night the day
> Thou canst not then be false to any man/Farewell,
> my blessing season
> This in thee![18]

This famous quote, many times recited, urges Laertes, his son, in being well-balanced. He urges him to be real and truthful with himself as he judges his very own deeds, to be honest with others in deed, and always to do the right thing. The quote is about self-actualization. Some scholars argue that "to thine own self be true" implies self-benefit. However, if the latter is Polonius's intent, the ego has great probability to gain control, resulting in narcissistic behavior in many instances.

Sigmund Freud's tripartite model of the mind is inclusive of the id, ego, and superego or "it," "I," and "above I." According to Freudian theory, ego is the psychological apparatus that regulates sexual and aggressive impulse and guides the tension between those impulses and the demands and values of society.[19] Modern psychology suggests that the ego is the self-consciousness system, which regulates the part of the human consciousness that mirrors one's thoughts, feelings, and actions. This system is responsible for inhibiting or justifying thoughts, feelings, and actions. Ultimately, ego is how one identifies. If the ego is related to meta-ethical moral relativism, moral value may be subject to the mental health status of an individual. As a routinely practiced habit, counselors ought to consider the decision-making capacity of counselees.

What are some historical consequences of meta-ethical moral relativism? Judges 21:25 (KJV) records, "In those days there was no king in Israel: every man did that which was right in his own eyes." This left Israel subject to *individualistic* governance according to self or tribal belonging. Samuel, who would later become prophet, priest, and judge over Israel, was born in Chapter 1 of 1 Samuel.[20] Israel's persistent battle with the Philistines served as a constant reminder that the Israelites were in need of a moral guide for crisis situations. As Samuel grew older, he appointed his sons as judges over Israel. His sons were given over to bribery, perverted judgment, and filthy lucre. The elders of Israel shared their concerns regarding the sons of Samuel and requested that he pray for a king to judge them. They wanted to be like other nations and have a king. At his displeasure, Samuel prayed. God commanded Samuel to hearken the voice of the people. God told Samuel that the people's request was not a rejection of Samuel but of God, Himself.[21] When a group of people or a person looks to itself for moral guidance, the group or the person may find a deficit or void. Like other meta-ethical moral relativists, Israel turned within herself for moral guidance. What a horrible mistake! Discovering moral guidance from the "self" who is *not* in internal conflict with itself is nearly impossible. A person with internal conflict will find it difficult to resolve nearly anything. The same is clear with Israel. Israel could not handle conflict within herself. The people of God needed a judge and spiritual guide in times of crisis or conflict. God sent Samuel but, like other nations, Israel wanted a king. They did not acknowledge the blessing of having Samuel whom God had given to them. Like an egoist, Israel wanted what suited "I" in the tripartite of Sigmund Freud's structural model of the psyche. Israelites thought having a king to judge them would result in an *identity or status* with other nations. The status of having a king would serve as the "id" or "it" necessary for them to have this identity among other nations or peers. The result is that the permissive will of God yielded them a king, Saul.

Saul, a very tall and stately guy from the tribe of Benjamin, presents another issue. While Saul was very good looking and stately outwardly, he was insecure inwardly. He stood physically above anyone else in Israel, yet he saw himself as a grasshopper. In 1 Samuel Chapter 9, Samuel goes to anoint Saul as king. Saul questions Samuel's efforts by stating that he is least of all being from the tribe of Benjamin.[22] This low view of "self" caused Saul to build a fortress of pride by which he felt his personal interests were protected. Trying to measure up against his own standards based on his erroneous perception of what he thought others thought of him, Saul stepped outside of his role as king and usurped the priestly office by offering a burnt offering. This act reveals one of several narcissistic behaviors attributed to Saul. He had no regard for God in his decision making. As long as he was winning and unashamed, Saul was fine. Saul was such a meta-ethical relativist that he was willing to be disobedient to God to foster his own agenda. He made a mistake that cost him his kingship in 1 Samuel 15.[23] As God had spoken to him, Samuel told Saul to smite Amalek and to "utterly" destroy it and slay the men, women, children, and mentioned livestock.[24] Instead, Saul was disobedient and spared King Agag and the choice portion of the livestock. He allows his personal wants to serve as a moral compass due to his insecurities and need to maintain status. The meta-ethical moral relativistic position can be harmful when embraced by the narcissist. One's selfishness does not always affect him or her alone, but it can be detrimental to others as well. Because of Saul's disobedience and his need to satisfy his own interests, the Jews could have been annihilated. His failure to follow through on God's command left King Agag alive. Had Agag and all the Amalekites been destroyed, Haman, the son of Hammedatha the Agagite, would not have been born to plot the destruction of the Jews.[25]

Let's visit what should have been paradise. The Garden of Eden became the scene of an egotistical showdown directed by the Serpent. God had instructed Adam and Eve not to eat the fruit of the tree in the midst of the garden.[26] Adam allowed the "id," his wants and desires, to win. Satan's lie would not have worked if Adam's desire was different and to please God. Instead, Adam believed the Serpent when he told him that his eyes would be opened and that he and Eve would be as gods having the knowledge of good and evil. When Eve ate and gave Adam to eat, their eyes were opened to their nakedness. According to the meta-ethical relativist, nakedness, here, is suggestive of the deficit often encountered when looking within one's self. Trying to walk the moral road alone will result in a devastating crisis when "self" becomes lost and cannot help "self" to find its way.

There are numerous books, podcasts, blogs, and campaigns which support the premise of personal pronouns. In other words, there is a big push for *self*-care, *self*-love, *self*-help, *self*-efficacy, and much more. Should self-love actually be feared rather than desired? In excess, it could lead to one traveling the tragic path of King Saul. When self-concept, who we are physically, spiritually, emotionally, socially, and otherwise, is obscured, the person who uses himself or herself as the standard for moral reasoning has no real standard at all.[27] Surely a healthy, whole, and balanced "self" is very important. However, the boundaries for which a healthy, whole, and balanced "self" exist are not well-defined. Perhaps, this definition is not well-defined because it, too, is relative to "self" and one's opinion. The Christian counselor may discover that self-assessment tools are a valuable part of the evaluative process. These tools can provide a scope of the counselee's perception of "self." Someone who is over-confident may not assume responsibility for his or her actions. His or her assigned value to morals may be considered, otherwise, as morally unstable. Someone who has a low view of "self," or low self-esteem, may assume responsibility when it is not theirs to own. This individual's view of "self" may lead them to assign higher moral value to others.

Normative Moral Relativism

Normative moral relativists contend that all moral views should be tolerated in the absence of a universal set of moral codes. This position attempts to normalize the gaps between moral value by acknowledging that although people or groups disagree, they should tolerate the views of others. How often do we see dysfunction being normalized? This is another unclear position on what moral value is. Does this mean the statement "when in Rome, do as the Romans do" holds true?[28] Or, does it mean that the Romans should allow the individual of another culture to do according to his or her own moral code while in Rome? Is toleration a matter of imposition prevention? Is the goal not to impose upon one another or be forced to consider another's view? This position is thought to be an *objective* approach to dealing with diverse cultural practices and traditions.

The Christian counselor's goal should not lie within objectivity alone. Biblical application may be compromised when "being objective" is the main goal of counseling. The normative moral relativistic position bespeaks this by suggesting toleration of an unagreeable behavior. Tolerance is the ability to endure a behavior or opinion that one does not necessarily agree with.[29] The Christian counselor must consider if he has the right to excuse sin. Proper consideration will always yield a "no." If the Bible is used as the standard for counseling, the counselor cannot subscribe to this position. The counselor should be especially mindful of his own Christian values being compromised when counseling someone who does not identify as a Christian. Again, the Holy Spirit must be a respected partner in counseling settings. While it is not wise to force anyone to salvation, the work of the Holy Spirit can provide the counselor with effective methods for ministering to the heart of the counselee. Paul urges that we allow every man to be fully persuaded in his own mind. In Romans 14:1–4, he warns against contention over what can be considered traditions and/or cultural practices of abstaining from or eating meat.[30] He notions that some of the things that birth contentions are morally indifferent. He warns against assigning any moral values at all to these indifferent things. If the emphasis is placed on these indifferences, the brother of weaker faith will focus on achieving in these indifferent areas rather than being a Christian loved by his brethren and by God. Paul urges the stronger brother to embrace the weaker brother with love. He discourages disputes of such cultural matters. Paul was dealing with the merging of the traditional Jews and newly converted Gentiles. He admonishes them not to highlight their differences which would not glorify God. Instead, he uses the gospel as a *common* ground for them to share what they had in common, which is a love for Jesus. Paul did not only labor to teach them to love God, but also to love one another. This passage demonstrates the meaning of tolerance, which binds and *does* not compromise. On the contrary, the normative moral relativists suggest being tolerant when there is no agreement at all. Paul is admonishing a group of people of different cultural backgrounds who are building from the same foundation, Jesus Christ. Paul is teaching them that Jesus is absolute, and all else is variable. Therefore, their cultural differences are not debatable, comparable, or measurable in reference to salvation and the onward growth of discipleship. Love became a consistent theme in the Pauline epistles as the gospel was preached to and accepted by Gentiles across the world. Gentiles were considered anyone who were not Jewish. The acceptance of Jesus Christ by the Gentiles and the acceptance of Gentiles by the Jews were two distinct phenomena. Because there were so many sub-cultures among the Gentiles, the Jews were constantly being taught "inclusion." The Jews had been known exclusively as God's people. Paul admonishes them in Ephesians 4:2 to respond with all humility, gentleness, patience, and to bear with one another in love.[31] Throughout the New Testament, he promotes brotherly love.

Businesses, corporations, and human resource management departments invest time and finances into sensitivity, diversity, and inclusion education and trainings for employees. Just as the Jews were to be openminded about receiving Gentile brothers and sisters, the Gentiles had to openminded about coming to the common ground as well. They had to be willing to give up their gods. The contender for normative moral relativism would argue that the Jews would need to tolerate these practices. There were some things the Jews, themselves, had to be open to in order to receive Jesus as the Messiah. The Holy Spirit had to be at the center of it all. Without Him, the hearts of the Jews or the Gentiles would not have been pliable enough to see Jesus as the center of it all. When Jesus becomes the focus, those who focus on Him become one corporately. Let's put that into perspective now. The answers to those challenges being faced by Americans and around the world are not rooted in political parties, skin color, or denominational affiliation for that matter. These things often are solved by how we handle matters of the heart.

On Mars' Hill, the Apostle Paul proclaimed the gospel to the people of Athens.[32] There he made observation of their superstitious practices. He declared unto them the nonsense of their worship "TO THE UNKNOWN GOD," as inscribed on the altar.[33] He goes on to tell them about the God who made the world and all things. Paul is not contradicting himself here in Acts 17 in contrast to what he stated in Romans 14. A comparative analysis of the two texts reveals a difference. The debate over meat in Romans 14 was useless and morally irrelevant. The worship of other gods presented a very distinguishably different issue. Eating meat did not dismiss Jesus Christ as the risen Savior, who alone should be worshipped. In Acts 17, the worship of other gods indicated a devotion issue. The Athenians could not be both committed to Jesus (God) and to gods created by their own hands. A lack of devotion subjects the audience to moral compromise. The gods could not and should not have been tolerated.

What about grace? Does grace allow for the tolerance suggested by proponents of normative moral relativism? Christian counselors must not fall into the trap of grace as a "guilt-trip." The divine grace of God is likened unto a camp of protection or a precious place in God. Jesus' death on Calvary demonstrated the grace of God in action. Paul, in his address to the church at Ephesus, says we are saved by grace through faith.[34] He goes on to say that our salvation is not of our own doing, but it is a gift of God.[35] If grace is the work of God (and it is), it cannot be used in the argument for normative moral relativism. Christian counselors should not view the extension of grace as a method for practicing tolerance. Paul poses a few questions in Roman 6:1–2 (KJV), "What shall we say then? Shall we continue in sin, that grace may abound? God forbid. How shall we, that are dead to sin, live any longer in it?" Paul is admonishing believers and new converts to have no fellowship with darkness; therefore, sin should not be tolerated.[36] When sin is identified in counseling, the counselor should not allow it to go without proper address. It is clear in Romans 6:2 that God does not mean for grace to be abused.[37]

Normative moral relativists seem to suggest abiding by the idiom, "going along to get along." Dr. Kyle Irwin, an assistant professor of sociology at Baylor University, says that conformity leads to positive feeling, attachments, solidarity.[38] He claims that these are what motivate people to continue their behavior. Exercising tolerance toward the moral codes of others could be considered by some as caving into social pressure. The result is more of the same behaviors. However, this trend can be of great value when the repeated behavior is desired. On the contrary, this trend can be of no value when there is a need for behavior modification. Neglecting the opportunity to do that which is right is a sin of omission. It is not enough to disagree with what is wrong. Right and wrong must be determined by a moral absolute. The moral relativist does not believe there is a universal or absolute standard for what is right or wrong. James, the half-brother of Jesus, warns that knowing what is right and not doing it is sin.[39] Christians must depend on the Holy Spirit's supply of wisdom when addressing moral issues. Failure to address sin can actually serve as a means of promoting it.

When moral choices are made without a moral guide other than self and/or a group of people sharing common culture and traditions, those who follow these choices are subject to themselves. The equivalent is self-coronation, the act of crowning one's self as the authority. Sir William Osler said, "A physician who treats himself has a fool for a patient."[40] Former President Abraham Lincoln stated something similar, "He who represents himself has a fool for a client."[41] Psalm 14:1 says that the fool has said within his heart there is no God.[42] He goes on to say that the work of the fool is corrupt and abominable.[43] In Christian counseling, the Word of God must serve as the absolute guide for determining right and wrong.

Idealistic Distortion versus Reality

Ideally, every Christian counselor's desire is for every counselee to gain biblical resolution and live a fulfilled life thereafter. Most people possess an idealistic view of what his or her life should be or look like. What happens when the ideal life is not realized? Can the ideal life be accomplished? The term idealistic is an adjective which describes that which is of high moral or intellectual value or that which is lofty and grandeur in some cases.[44] Someone who is idealistic is thought of as one who is often referred to as a perfectionist, romantic, or optimist. This individual sees his or her desires in an exalted presence. Unfortunately, life is not an autobiography acted out on a perfect scenery that when flawed can be rewritten to agree with our ideals and expectations. How much of counseling is actually spent tearing down the false expectations that the counselee may have erected for "self?" Like a meticulous and skilled, plan-driven surgeon, the counselor is responsible for preserving hope in the counselee while allowing room for the work of the Holy Spirit to demolish false expectations. If left unaddressed, idealistic views can blind the counselee to his reality. Blinded by what is idealistic, the counselee does not have the power to make shifts in his reality to accomplish the right goals. For this reason, it is beneficial in the counseling session to contrast what is ideal with that which is real. These practices may prove beneficial for parents desiring to relate to their children who may have their own set of ideals contradictory to the desires of the parents.

The realist, in contrast to the idealist, is a person who accepts a situation as is and is prepared to deal with it accordingly.[45] Unlike the idealist who metaphorically has a pencil with an eraser ready to rewrite the perfect ending, the realist sees his story penned in ink. The realist is not without need for counseling. Often the realist lives with an "it is what it is" notion. This resigned acceptance of what is does not promote change in any direction forward. A realist may not agree with the status quo but will deal with it as it is. The counselor's role is to allow the counselee to deal with the reality while allowing the work of the Holy Spirit for building a new and better construct. If allowed to continue thinking according to his own position, neither the idealist nor the realist will attain. The realist will accept what is and spend his or her energy dealing with the situation as is. The idealist will live in a self-customized utopia, wasting energy on what may never happen and possibly on what should not ever happen.

A robustly built assessment tool can be used to survey what is called social conditioning. Conditioning is the process of training or accustoming a person to behave a certain way or to accept certain circumstances. By exploring the cultural practices and traditions of a counselee, the Christian counselor can make some inferences regarding environmental factors, religious beliefs or disbeliefs, demographics, and other factors responsible for conditioning the counselee. The counselor considers how these factors may have shaped and even distorted the thoughts and position of the individual seeking help.

Prepare/Enrich is one of the most widely researched assessment tools used to evaluate and conduct research on relationships.[46] The company uses a tool called the idealistic distortion score to assess the tendency for individuals to respond to statements in a socially desirable manner. The tool is used to measure the extent to which a person distorts their relationship in a positive direction. The assessment tool considers three areas of idealistic distortion: very high idealistic distortion, moderate idealist distortion, and low idealistic distortion.

Very High Idealistic Distortion

A score of 85% or above suggests that an individual is invested in presenting his or her relationship in a highly favorable manner.[47] This person may not be willing to acknowledge or address problem areas in the relationship. He may be willing to view things through a rose-colored lens. The rose-colored glasses idiom is an optimistic perception of something or a positive opinion with regard. This individual has a customized view of how he or she perceives the relationship. Their desired perception is the only thing in view. This position should be concerning to the counselor. The counselor cannot allow this person room to guide and or manipulate the counseling session. If allowed to do so, the counselee will direct everything in the favor of his or her desires. Premarital counseling cannot serve as a "check-off" before marriage. The process should be conducted without compromise of the truth.

Moderate Idealistic Distortion

A score of 40-60% suggests that the individual has moderate idealist distortion.[48] Married couples are usually identified in this category. It is easily assumable that married couples who are generally not in a troubled marriage plot here. Couples who have invested time and assets into the marriage may see those investments as ideal reasons to score within the 40-60% range regardless of other realities which may not be ranked well.

Low Idealistic Distortion

A score of 0-30% suggests that the individual has a realistic view of his or her relationship rather than an idealistic one.[49] This individual is more likely to be open to discussing problems. The counselor should help the individual and/or the couple to look at the existing problems and work toward any possible resolution. Often, the identified problems are viewed as small things. If left unaddressed, these small things have great potential to destroy a marriage. A low idealist distortion correlates directly with a high realistic view of the relationship. Couples who are in troubled marriages tend to fall into this category. These couples are usually at a place where they are not attempting to give socially desirable responses.

When dealing with relativists, idealists, or realists, the Christian counselor should depend on the Holy Spirit for guidance. The infallible Word of God must be respected as a trusted source among other counseling and assessment tools. The Word must be interpreted and applied without cultural or individual bias. Christian counselors must be fully persuaded that what God has promised, He is also able to perform.[50] Therefore, it is not the job of the counselor to manufacture miracles or make anything happen. It is the responsibility of the counselor to invite the presence of the Holy Spirit. It is His work that will produce change, repentance, and miracles. The counselor must be convinced that all scripture is inspired by God and profitable for teaching, for reproof, for correction, and for training in righteousness.[51]

PART II

COMPASSIONATE CHRISTIAN COUNSELING AND ITS APPLICATION

CHAPTER 3

COMPASSIONATE CHRISTIAN COUNSELING ROOTED IN LOVE

For the Christian believer, the Word of God is absolute and God, Himself, is the absolute authority. The Christian counselor is distinguished from all others by this same principle. Though the Christian counselor may esteem God as the absolute authority and the holy scripture as the authoritative truth, he or she must acknowledge that this belief is not universal in the world. There are those people who profess to believe in God but believe that moral value is relative. In addition to moral relativists, there are those who believe that moral value is situational. No matter where a person falls within the spectrum of morality, the Christian counselor must be willing to accept where the counselee is. This acceptance does not mean the two have to agree initially or at all.

Dr. R. Y. Langham defines Christian counseling as biblical counseling and Christian psychology which combines your faith with the principles of psychology to improve mental health and relationships.[52] Langham states that this therapy approach uses scripture and biblical teachings to help counselees deal with life's challenges.[53] Others define Christian counseling and biblical counseling as set apart and distinctively different. Dr. Jay Adams, founder of the Institute of Nouthetic Studies, advocates that the

Bible is the most trusted source for counseling needs.[54] His approach includes three confrontation elements: confrontation happening in a face-to-face manner; confrontation done out of loving concern for the counselee; and confrontation done with the purpose of bringing change that God desires.[55] Some Christian counselors may think of the nouthetic-biblical approach suggested by Dr. Adams as a radical one. Dr. Adams is leading the movement for Christian counselors to divorce unbiblical psychological theory and renew confidence in the power of the Holy Spirit. We have explored Sigmund Freud's theory which, seemingly, is intellectual psychology but is spiritually and nouthetically void. Freud's theory is spiritually fraud. It supports the idea satisfying "self" rather than pleasing God. Adams warns against mixing theory and theology.

For the sake of discussion here, the Christian counselor is considered as one who believes the Word of God as a distinguished truth which sanctifies.[56] The Christian counselor is also one who applies biblical truths and leans on the Holy Spirit for wise counsel. It is important to note that the Christian counselor and the counselor who is a Christian are not one in the same. As prior mentioned, the Christian counselor intentionally relies upon and uses the scriptures as material for counseling the counselee. In contrast, the counselor *who is a Christian* may share his or her Christian experience without *intentionally* incorporating the Word of God or *intentionally* including the Holy Spirit in the counseling process.

The Case for the Word in Counseling

The Christian believes that God is creator of all mankind. So, why would man know more than God about His creation? Genesis tells the story of Creation and gives a description of the first surgery as Adam is put to sleep and Eve is created.[57] God told Jeremiah that He knew him before He even formed him in his mother's womb.[58] Isaiah 64:8 compares creation unto clay in the Potter's hand.[59] Paul refs to mankind as God's workmanship created in Christ Jesus for good works, which He (God) prepared beforehand that we should walk in them.[60] There is something to be said about the hand of God in counseling. Most people seeking counseling are broken or torn within. These individuals are seeking a way to mend their brokenness or simply to pick up the pieces. The Christian counselor understands that while we were, yet sinners Christ died for us.[61] He purchased us with His blood and made us free.[62] When someone purchases a product or an item which needs assembling, the item will more likely come with the manufacturer's guide and/or instructions for putting things together. At the time of assembly, all the details of the manufacturer's guide may not be needed. As time progresses, the owner of the item may refer to the manual for minor repair. The Holy Spirit, who is God, knows about the creation. Remember that the Holy Spirit was there when God decided to make Adam. Genesis 1:26 (KJV) says, "And God said, 'Let *us* make man in *our* image, after *our* likeness: and let them have dominion over the fish of the sea, and over the fowl of the air, and over the cattle, and over all the earth, and over every creeping thing that creepeth upon the earth.'" (emphasis mine) He knows how to put the counselee back together again. Why not respect the Holy Spirit as an ally in counseling? The Christian counselor who endeavors to counsel with compassion, yet without compromise, should seek to do well in his or her own living. King David warns believers not to receive counsel from the ungodly nor to stand in the way of sinners.[63] The latter can have dual interpretative value. Counselors should consider that their engagement in acts of sin can be a hinderance to those who are observing. The Christian counselor can further glean from King David's advice to meditate on the Word of the Lord day and night.[64] By doing so, he or she will become more grounded in the Word as opposed to leaning to his or her own understanding. Self-reliance is a common threat for both the counselor and the counselee. The Apostle Paul cautions that the foolishness of God is wiser than men and the weakness of God is stronger than men.[65] The case for God in counseling is indisputable. The Holy Spirit has the advantage of knowing both the counselor and the counselee. He knows us better than we know ourselves and constantly intercedes on our behalf.[66] Any counsel aside from the guidance of the Holy Spirit compromises the value of counseling and compromises the application of the gospel. Wisdom is but for a time in the world, but it is for an eternity with God. The Spirit of God places us in touch with God's wisdom. He explores the depths of God and reveals those things which are not superficial.[67] Psychologists, psychiatrists, and those who do not incorporate the Word of God may only deal with the portion of the glacier easily seen above water. The existing portion of that glacier underwater may be underestimated for its depth and width. Only the Holy Spirit can explore the deep things of God and the hidden issues of mankind. The Holy Spirit, God, knows the eternal life ahead. Without the help of the Holy Spirit, any "said" successful counseling outcomes are only temporarily so. Theories will be revised, and many will even fail. However, the Word of God is without revision and stands tried and true. Theories–like the grass–will wither, concepts–like the flower–will fade, but the Word of God will remain.[68] Christian counseling, contrary to popular belief, deals with the whole man. It is applicable to more than faith-based principles and psychological issues. The Apostle Paul's plea for the people at Thessalonica was that the God of peace sanctify them completely or wholly and that their whole spirit, soul, and body be kept blameless at the coming of the Lord.[69]

In John 1, the Word of God is personified. Verse 1 says, "In the beginning was the Word, and the Word was with God, and the Word was God."[70] Jesus is God. The counselee who believes in the living Word has access through Him to better counseling outcomes. Throughout the gospels, the Word, *Jesus*, works. Jesus, the living Word, told the woman with the issue of blood that her faith made her whole.[71] He asked the man lying at the Pool of Bethesda if he wanted to be made whole.[72] Jesus was not simply interested in having an encounter that would heal their diseases.

His complete work on Calvary affords us an opportunity not only to be healed of our infirmities, but also to be restored to whole life or eternal life. Christian counselors should pray for the miracle of salvation for those counselees who do not believe Jesus is Lord. Jesus told His disciples that they would engage in what I refer to as the "greater works anointing."[73] Christian counselors should embrace the concept of discipleship and endeavor for the greater works to be accomplished. Jesus promised that He would leave a Comforter or Advocate, the Holy Spirit. He is the trusted advocate who aids in doing the greater works. The works are given by God to be accomplished by Him through those who submit to His power and authority. When Jesus made His ascension to be with His Father, the disciples were trusted with the task of continuing with the kingdom's agenda. The Acts of the Apostles would have been nullified without the work of the Holy Spirit. God is the same yesterday, today, and forever.[74] He wants people whole. His death gives access to that which is eternal so that those who believe and trust Him do not have to settle for what is temporary.

Love Works

What's love got to do with it? Jesus would probably respond with a very simple reply, "Everything." Jesus manages to use that which is exclusive to be inclusive. The love of God is so exclusive because it is incomparable and full of compassion. Nothing parallels to the authentic love of God. This "one of a kind" love has an inexplicable drawing power which is hospitable and covers a multitude of faults.[75] The essence of love flows in His shed blood that while we were sinners, He died for every one of us. Biochemists settle that blood is a connective tissue.[76] It connects all the organ systems and removes wastes from them as well. In its normal, unseparated form, it is adhesive and salty.[77] Salt has the tendency to draw electrolytes in the physical body. It influences the directions that these substances flow. Jesus' work on Calvary and His bloodshed definitely connects the relationship between the spiritual self and the physical self. Blood is our life-giving supply. Jesus shed His blood for the remission of sins and the atonement of mankind. His work on Calvary provides access to connect us back to God. The beauty of the blood of Jesus is that it also connects people to *one another*. In Matthew 5:13, Jesus calls His disciples the salt of the earth.[78] How does this relate to counseling? The Christian counselor should have the character of God. That godly character working in tandem with the guidance of the Holy Spirit has great potential for producing successful outcomes. Someone may wonder what empirical data is there to support such premise. The real question is how can empirical data deny the work of one who conquered death, hell, and the grave? Empirical data does not compare to the providential hand of God. Jay Adams's unapologetic response to such line of questioning is as follows:

> "Since the human counselor is not the only one who is at work in Christian counseling, the Christian has an 'unfair advantage' over other counselors. With the Holy Spirit enlightening the minds of counselees and enabling them to overcome sinful propensities that hinder growth, producing His fruit through His inerrant Word, what profit would there be in trying to determine how well a human counselor counsels? In effect, he is but a catalyst, ministering the Scriptures in ways that the Spirit utilizes to bring about change in counselees. The Spirit is the ultimate Counselor. The whole concept of empirical evidence, statistics and the like, begs the question. And the thought of attempting to obtain them is repugnant. Sorry, but that is how it is."[79]

Attempts to be "legitimized" in the role of a Christian counselor are futile. The Holy Spirit is enough. That does not mean that other counseling tools are rejected by the Christian counselor. It means that the Holy Spirit is superior. With this prioritization of the Holy Spirit, it is likely that counseling will be delivered with compassion and void of compromise.

The true meaning of love is centered around Calvary. Jesus' work on Calvary resulted in victory over sin. However, the victory would not have been attainable had there been compromise. The passion of Christ was evident in His suffering. No greater love has been demonstrated before or after Christ gave His life as a ransom for sin.[80] The Christian counselor, as do other Christians, must respond to the call to greater works noted in John 14:12–14. Again, Jesus tells his disciples that they will do greater works. Counseling is part of those greater works. What could be more befitting in a time of suffering than to be introduced to and have fellowship with the Holy Spirit? The Christian counselor must be willing to present the Truth without compromise but instead with love.

John 3:16

Calvary happened because of God's love. God did not love from a place of willful blindness concerning man's sin. Aware of the frail and sinful state of man, He yet chose to love intentionally and with great purpose. The grace of God is such an apparent intent and theme of John 3:16 (KJV), "For God so loved the world that He gave His only begotten Son that whosoever believeth on Him should not perish but shall have everlasting life." Of course, the work of God's grace produces everlasting life and reconciliation. However, it is worth it to look at the intent which led to the overall mission being accomplished. The common goal of every Christian counselor for every counselee is to make sure that the counselee's relationship with God is intact. This is discipleship at its best. If the counselee does not have a relationship with God, the counselor has an opportunity for sharing the gospel of Jesus. A word of caution should be offered with regard. The decision for salvation of the unbelieving counselee is not in the power of the counselor. The Christian counselor's job is to be obedient to and dependent on the leading of the Holy Spirit. The Holy Spirit will do the work.

"So" Loved

"For God so loved the World" is such a pregnant statement.[81] This portion of scripture expresses the intensity of God's love and to whom it was directed. The word, "so," reveals the intentional character and nature of God. He was intentional about what He did because of "so" loving the World. This expression speaks to the depth, length, and width of God's indescribable, unexplainable, far-reaching, love for mankind.[82] He did not allow anything other than love to be the deciding factor for His sacrifice. He did not care about the categorizing labels that separate people into subgroups which only result in further fragmentation of both members of the body of Christ and of individuals at the core of their being. Just as the blood serves as connective tissue in the physical body, the blood of Jesus serves as a binder, creating a bond of unity for us. He restores life to the spiritually and emotionally depleted areas of life just as blood replenishes the physically anemic areas.

The Christian counselor should aim to follow the example of God more than following a plan of counseling. Certainly, a plan is good to have and should not be negated. However, the plan is only as good as the one who devises it. Biblical counseling, used interchangeably but referring to use of the Bible, provides the counselee with a path for recovery or reconciliation based on biblical principles. God, Himself, declares that He knows the plans He has toward us to prosper, not harm, and to give a future to whoever will receive Him.[83] How can the counselor be part of that plan? One way is by promoting the need for connecting with God. If the counselee has a disconnect from God, the counselor should share uncompromisingly, yet lovingly, the need for God. The other way is to help the counselee embrace the need to connect with the "right" others. The "right" others are those people who are connected to God as well. The scripture talks about the need for fellowship and the power of one another.[84] This power of one another is found in unity. Paul urges the church at Ephesus to endeavor to keep the unity of the Spirit in the bond of peace. In Ephesians Chapter 4, he declares that there is one body, one Spirit, one Lord, one faith, one baptism, and one God who is father of all.[85] The oneness and unity referred to in this chapter is made possible through Christ Jesus' atonement. Uncompromised, compassionate Christian counseling is not designed to judge the counselee, but through love encourage repentance or the courage to change directions. John poses the question about truly loving God. He questions how one can say he loves God who he has never seen yet hate his brother who he has seen?[86] Jesus balanced loving the sinner and hating sin. He still loves today with the same objective of connecting with sinners as He did in the home of Zacchaeus. Jesus worked at getting people to commune together. If counseling is to be without compromise, it must also be without discrimination. Self-righteousness and pride must be guarded against by all Christians. If the counselor is not vigilant concerning the two, these evils will take a leisurely stroll into the counseling session. Opinions should not be given by the counselor in exchange for the loving delivery of God's Word.

Whosoever

God's love is further illustrated in that He gave His *only* [Son] for *whosoever.* God did not reserve His love for a special group of people of a certain economic, ethnic, social, religious, culture, gender, or age group. He gave His life without any reservation of who would receive new life as a result of receiving Him. Christian counselors must realize that Christian people will not be the only people who will or need to opt for Christian services and/or counseling. To deny counseling to unbelievers based on their unbelief does not reflect the love of God evidenced in John 3:16. Christ loved the world so much that He extended an invitation that still stands open today. Everyone does not accept the invitation at the same time. Christ extended that invitation over two thousand years ago, and it has been a standing invitation for "whosoever." As Christians, we cannot choose our assignments. Therefore, the Christian counselor cannot always choose the "comfortable" work. Remember Jonah? The Lord gave him an assignment, and he disobeyed. Jonah 1:2–3 (KJV) says, "Arise, go to Nineveh, that great city, and cry against it; for their wickedness is come up before me. But Jonah rose up to flee unto Tarshish from the presence of the Lord, and went down to Joppa; and he found a ship going to Tarshish: so, he paid the fare thereof, and went down into it, to go with them unto Tarshish from the presence of the Lord."

Understand that whosoever means "whosoever." Whosoever, a formal term of whoever, is a pronoun referring to a person, or people. It is indiscriminate. Christian counselors who seek to do the will of God will be open to counsel whosoever. They will not run away from the assignment. Great debate can form around this premise. Counselors must not limit counseling to what *they* can do. When the Holy Spirit is incorporated into the setting of counseling, there are great possibilities for what can happen even in the seemingly toughest of cases. What is impossible with man is possible with God.[87] God did not send His only begotten Son to die for a people who have no potential to receive Him as Lord. *Whosoever* believes in Him can have eternal life. Any person can be described by the term "whosoever." No one gains eternal life without first accepting Jesus as Lord.[88] Again, Jesus died for sinners in our *sinful* state. Love led the mission which was accomplished at Calvary. As a child of God made in His image and commissioned to go and teach all nations and baptize them, the Christian counselor must be intentional about seeing the potential of those in need of help.[89] Love must serve as the lens through which others are viewed by any Christian, especially Christian counselors.

The indiscriminate love of Jesus Christ is without borders and limitation. It goes to the deepest and darkest places in search of "whosoever." The task of the Christian counselor is rooted in being compassionate without condemnation of the counselee and compromise of the gospel of Jesus Christ. This task cannot be completed without love. Being intentional in love is so important. Counselors and other Christian leaders must be committed to speaking the truth in love.[90] In a world where political and cultural correctness coupled with sensitivity practices are stressed in every institution, the precautionary reaction of professionals is to be accommodative by compromise. The precautionary reaction of the Christian counselor, unlike others, is *not* to be so accommodative that he or she risks compromising the gospel. Paul asked the church at Galatia if he was their enemy for telling them the truth.[91] The question posed is a rhetorical one. Christian counselors should not be given over to the likeness of judaistic teachers of the Bible. The judaistic teachers were trying to win over the Galatians for their benefit. Paul warned the Galatians that they would only be flattered by the heretical teachers. Interestingly, he further warned them that to depend on the judaistic teachers would leave them subject to their control and approval. Winning the approval of the counselor is not the goal of biblical or Christian counseling. The goal is for the counselee to gain the approval of God, which comes by His grace. Paul's teachings were designed to bring them to understand the grace of God and its liberating power from the grip of religiosity and ceremonial law. If counselees gain understanding of the true essence of grace, they will be inspired to live freely for God. Grace has a functional duality:

- It gives "whosoever" free access.
- It releases the counselee from the control of meritocracy.

Compromise of the gospel disrupts the path between God and counselee. If he or she is to see the handywork of the Omnipotent One and connect with Him, the counselor must not water down the potency of the Word.

Potent Blood vs. Unstable Water

In Genesis 49, Jacob speaks prophetic blessings upon his sons. He began with Reuben, his first-born. The blessing initially sounds like nothing but adoration as Jacob referred to Reuben as his might, the beginning of his strength, the excellency of dignity, and the excellency of power.[92] What follows is nothing shy of a plot twister. Jacob proceeded on to describe Reuben as "unstable as water."[93] Jacob told his son that he would not excel. Because of sin, he could not excel. Charles Spurgeon says, "So a man may have great opportunities, and yet lose them. Uncontrolled passions may make him very little who otherwise might have been great."[94] Reuben defiled the bed of his father, and it cost him. How could someone mighty, full of strength with the excellency of dignity and power, be unstable as water? His sin ruined the future of the tribe. No prophets, judges, or kings are recorded as rising from the Tribe of Reuben. Molecularly, water is known for its weak hydrogen bonds to oxygen. The weak bonds are easily broken. Sin has the same effect on the relationship between us and God. Sin separates the sinner from God. Therefore, no "watered- down" solution will work in counseling. If the issue facing the counselee revolves around the need for repentance, the need to forgive, or to be forgiven, a lukewarm version of what is right will not work. God longs for a people who are resolute –hot or cold– not lukewarm.[95]

Again, Jesus told His disciples that they would do greater works in John 14:12–14. In verse 15, He said, "If you love me, you will keep my commandments."[96] This statement marries the need for compassion without compromise. Disciples are to love the Lord. Again, how can we love the Lord and not love the one we see? To love God is to love others. In counseling, the counselor must love God enough to love the counselee. The counselor is responsible to keep the commandments of God and to urge the counselee to do so. This further supports the claim that counseling must be done without compromise of the gospel. Jesus' statement also confirms that love and compromise cannot occupy the same. Some would disagree. Practicing patience and compromising are two different things. Compromise is an agreement where concessions are made by both sides. Patience is a virtue that allows the counselor to accept delay until the counselee reaches the godly resolve he or she needs. Patience does not negate the Word of God.

The potency of the Word of God should not be diluted by the opinions and comfort levels of the counselor or the counselee. The Word of God is quick, powerful, and sharper than any two-edged sword, piercing even to the dividing asunder of the soul and spirit, and the joints and marrow, and is a discerner of the thoughts and intents of the heart.[97] Though fluid, not even water can penetrate the impermeable membrane of God's Word. His Word is true and tried. God could have required for all mankind to be washed with water baptism as the method for restoration. Water was not enough. That which connects and flows to every part of the body was necessary. A blood sacrifice was required. Water, alone, does not give a man life. Water will not sustain the heart of man. Blood is the requirement to change the heart of man. Just as blood is essential for the physical sustainability of mankind, so the blood is essential for bringing man to repentance and reconciliation with the Father. The duality of Jesus, as fully man and fully God, is literally at the center of His heart. Jesus, a man who bore a human heart and who is God, shed His blood that human beings would be able to repent and have circumcised hearts for Him. Only the blood of Jesus could accomplish this great feat. No cardiothoracic surgeon, psychologist, and/or psychiatrist, no matter how skilled, could have accomplished the miracle at Calvary. Without the shedding of blood there is no remission of sin.[98] Therefore, a watered-down view of the scripture will not enhance the lives of the counselees. They must be brought to a self-awareness regarding sin and to the reality of living in obedience to the Word of God.

CHAPTER 4

THE ROLE OF THE CHRISTIAN COUNSELOR

The role and job description of the Christian counselor is dependent upon the definition one embraces regarding a Christian counselor. For the sake of discussion here, the Christian counselor is one who depends on the Word of God as the standard for counseling and the Holy Spirit as a compass. The Christian counselor is different from the *counselor who is a Christian*. The counselor who is Christian may choose to counsel based on cultural respects for the counselee in addition to the use of psychology. He or she may choose to retain his or her own beliefs while adhering to the boundaries of the counselee. However, the *Christian counselor*, as opposed to the counselor who is a Christian, does not adhere to moral relativistic views of the counselee. Some commentators believe there is a difference between *Christian* and *biblical counseling*. In this discussion, the two are used interchangeably. How can one truly promote Christian counseling aside from the Bible? Other commentators believe that the incorporation of psychology weakens biblical or Christian counseling. This is relative to the counselor. To absolutely believe that counselors cannot incorporate psychology into the realm of counseling is to believe that psychologists cannot be Christians. This cannot be stated absolutely here.

Therapy and Theology or Therapy versus Theology

The debate continues in respect to therapy and theology. Rather than questioning if therapy and theology are antagonists, the question should be asked when are they antagonists and when are they protagonists. The Christian counselor who decides to incorporate psychology as a source for counseling should maintain the premise that the Word of God is superior to any source and that the Holy Spirit's guidance is indisputable. The Holy Spirit helps with the discerning of spirits. Psychology is no competitor with the Holy Spirit; however, I believe that it can assist in counseling. The Holy Spirit provides discernment and reveals the plot of the enemy. The scripture reveals that God's people should not be ignorant of the enemy's devices; thereby, providing him an advantage.[99] Paul was talking in relation to unforgiveness and the need to forgive. However, it also holds true that believers should be wise as serpents and harmless as doves.[100] It is, therefore, advantageous to the Christian to know what the worldview is. Knowing this view does not mean that the counselor agrees with it. The counselor should be able to identify it to address it correctly. To believe that God is Creator and to reject scientific data is questionable. God, Creator of heaven and earth, knows the very atomic basis of mankind. Can God heal chemical imbalances in the brain? Certainly, He can. How will the counselor pray effectively for the chemical imbalance if it is left unidentified simply because it lay under the subtitle of some branch of science? Christian counseling does not need to be affirmed by the sciences. Do not get lost here. If the Christian counselor uses the sciences as an affirmation for counseling, a problem can easily ensue. In short, therapy cannot affirm theology, but theology can affirm or disaffirm therapy. Therapy is not always theologically sound, but proper theology is therapeutic when adhered to and applied appropriately.

Sigmund Freud, an atheist neurologist and the said founder of psychoanalysis, viewed religion as a pathology. Freud's theory with concern to personality and the interaction of three components of the mind (the id, ego, and superego) is worth knowing as a Christian counselor. While Christians should not submit to the "self" theory, knowing about this theory can assist with understanding things from the counselee's point of view. Understanding the counselee's perspective can be helpful when conducting a needs assessment. It is important to note that Freud's theory does not stand morally. It suggests an inward solution is available for the counselee. How can a *flawed* "self" give a plausible solution for itself? Note here that some individuals receiving counseling may not be filled with the Holy Spirit. So that we do not get hung up with denominational beliefs, let me say it this way. Not everyone receiving counseling has invited Christ into their heart. Consideration of Freud's viewpoint reveals another issue worth exploring, the pathology of religion especially as it relates to Christianity.

The Pathology of Religion

While some argue whether religion is enough, it is important to consider when or if religion is *too* much. The basis for this argument lies within the ambiguous definition of religion. For some, the definition of religion encompasses more than the centrality of Calvary and Jesus Christ. As a matter of fact, neither Jesus nor Calvary may be at the center of many religions. Freud, who spoke particularly about fundamentalist Christians, viewed religion as a pathology.[101] Undoubtedly, religious abuse has been the platform for control and unfair treatment throughout history. However, all religious practices cannot be synonymously categorized. Many Christians are choosing not to consider themselves as religious, but instead as relational or as having a *relationship* with God. This distinction is often made to denounce the horrible historical ramifications of religious abuse, which have resulted in control and enslavement in many cases. The Christian counselor cannot be afraid to examine the crossroad of religion and psychosis. Yes, psychosis. When is faith no longer faith but the strong desire for one's personal wishes to be granted? Christian leaders and counselors must not fret because of nonbelievers like Freud who place the Word of God on trial. We must believe that the Word will prove infallible and able to withstand any test. Paul warned the Galatians of the religious abuse of many teachers. In I John 4:1–6 we are warned not to believe every spirit but to test the spirits to see whether they be of God.[102] We are further warned that many false prophets have gone throughout the world.[103] Religion should not be presented in counseling as a set of rules with conditional consequences. However, those who we counsel should not be misled into believing there are no consequences attached to actions. Presenting religion as a set of rules with daunting consequences nullifies the ministry of grace and may also discourage the counselee. As a result, the counselee may not be open to the work of the Holy Spirit and could easily be thrown into the meritorious system of thinking that what he or she *does* will save his or her soul.

Paul expressed the need to move away from the observation of special days and practices which had no power to save. He promoted Christianity not as a *practice* but as a *lifestyle*. Much of religion is rooted in faith-distorting behaviors which mimic (if not serve as) magic, sorcery, and witchcraft. Christian counselors should be alert concerning practices and beliefs which connect the counselee to wickedness such as occultism, divination, horoscopes, palm-reading, hypnotisms, necromancy, and similar acts.

Freud's attack on religion, when viewed objectively by the Christian, actually serves to strengthen and aid the practicing Christian counselor by allowing him or her to have a heightened awareness of religious misuse and abuse. Unfortunately, some people, deeply steeped in religious expectations, believe that suffering is related to the presence of sin. Counselors should not exclude suffering as a part of the Christian experience. The central dogma of Christianity revolves around the monotheistic God, the Father,

Son, and the Holy Spirit and the life, *death*, and resurrection of Jesus Christ. Suffering is a necessary part of how the Christian relates to God. In times of suffering, faith proves to be essential. In Chapter 3 of Philippians, the Apostle Paul, who was an intellect and scholar among scholars, said that he counted all things as rubbish in exchange to know the excellency of God. [104] Paul was willing to get rid of every practice and those so-called things on which he had formerly depended. Contrary to Freud's assertion regarding the "self," Paul rejected righteousness of his own self that he may, through faith in Christ, enjoy righteousness based on faith in Christ and not himself. He yearned to lose even that which had formerly seemed fruitful so that he would know the Lord and the power of His resurrection and the fellowship of His sufferings. [105]

When faith in God is misrepresented as a means for getting *one's* desired results, several terrible things can happen. When the counselee's desires are not met and the outcome is different from his or her expectation, he or she may totally dismiss God and/or religion altogether. The other issue with faith being presented as a means to an end rather than a continual relationship with God is that the counselee may not form a relationship with God; but instead, he or she will possess "faith" based upon material things and a desired outcome. The Book of Acts records that Simon the sorcerer believed and was baptized. [106] An area of precaution must be noted here. The thought should be pondered what did he believe *for*? Did Simon believe God for salvation or for power? When he saw the work of the Holy Spirit through the disciples, he offered to pay for it so he could lay hands on people and see them receive the Holy Ghost. Simon had not received the Holy Ghost himself! He had not submitted himself. Peter, uncompromisingly and without hesitation, addressed him firmly. [107] Quickly, Peter admonished Simon to repent. [108] Simon repented and asked Peter to pray for him. The role of the Christian counselor is like that of Peter, to stand firm in the Word.

Counselees should be instructed that the Holy Spirit is not the equivalent to a "Simon Says" game, whereby instructions are given to the Holy Spirit and He performs at the will of man. Our relationship with God is not abracadabra or hocus pocus. I often hear demanding prayers commanding God to do according to the desire of the one praying. This is selfish. Our prayers should align with biblical teachings. We should receive instructions from the Holy Spirit and commit to following His command...not the other way around. As I mentioned before, salvation and living the Christian life are matters of the heart. The counselee cannot say *right* things for the *wrong* reason and expect that deliverance will follow. For an example, let us look at the work of divination witnessed in Acts 16:16–20 (KJV),

> "And it came to pass, as we went to prayer, a certain damsel possessed with a spirit of divination met us, which brought her masters much gain by soothsaying: The same followed Paul and us, and cried, saying, These men are the servants of the most high God, which shew unto us the way of salvation. And this did she many days. But Paul, being grieved, turned and said to the spirit, I command thee in the name of Jesus Christ to come out of her. And he came out the same hour. And when her masters saw that the hope of their gains was gone, they caught Paul and Silas, and drew them into the marketplace unto the rulers, And brought them to the magistrates, saying, These men, being Jews, do exceedingly trouble our city,"

Here, the apostles are being followed by a damsel. She said all the right things about the men of God. However, her sayings were not in approval of their work or to the glory of God; but instead, for the profit of men. She had followed Paul for several days before he, being vexed by her ongoing and sayings, decided to address her. Paul, like Peter, did not hesitate in his confrontation of the spirit which guided her. This further proves that psychology cannot affirm Christian counseling. This passage helps us to understand that one counseling session may not be enough for a full and thorough assessment of the counselee. It further supports the claim that counselors need the Holy Spirit's guidance. The revelation shared by the Holy Spirit with Paul and the discernment he used are superior to any psychological theory.

Counseling the Unbeliever

The American Institute of Health Care Professionals, the AIHCP, is an organization which helps counselors with Christian beliefs to obtain a certification in Christian Counseling to better serve clients who are considered "spiritual."[109] Spiritual, in this context, refers to those who believe in the help of the Holy Spirit and the need for Christian counseling. What about those clients who may not fit the category of spiritual clients? Can *Christian* counseling benefit the *unbeliever*? Unbeliever, here, refers to anyone who does not believe that Jesus is the Son of God and that He is the only Way to be reconciled to the Father. There are times when those seeking help for mental disturbances desire not to be labeled by a diagnostic code and will seek Christian counseling as an alternative to traditional psychology or psychiatry. Many unbelievers who have the desire not to be labeled may opt for Christian counseling as an escape from the stigma associated with other means of professional help. No matter the reason for people seeking Christian counseling, the *Christian* counselor must consider the need for evangelism based upon the counselee's status as a believer or unbeliever in Jesus Christ. Let's discuss evangelism in counseling.

Evangelism in Counseling

Dr. Jay Adams suggests that the counselor should determine if the need for evangelism is indicated *prior* to beginning counseling.[110]

Dr. Ab Abercrombie, with the Biblical Counseling Institute, argues that the course and nature of counseling can only be determined within the counseling setting, where the Word and the Holy Spirit direct the counselor's assessment of the spiritual needs of the counselee.[111] He further suggests that without proper assessment in the counseling setting, the counselor is left to trust the counselee's representation of spiritual status without biblical examination. He cautions against this because many churchgoers bear a false security of salvation or the like based upon "human markers," such as baptism, confirmation, church membership, or church experience. He advises assessing whether the assignment or role of the counselor is restorative (bringing one back from a backslidden state) or evangelistic (salvation). If the counselee is found to have a relationship with Jesus, the role of the counselor is thought to be restorative. If the counselee does not have a relationship with Jesus, the role of the counselor is *evangelistic*. The counselor should assess the counselee's orientation of biblical truths for determination of his or her role in counseling the counselee. The assessment is a necessary part of Christian counseling because many still believe that rituals and traditions are the path to salvation. Like many Jews at the time of Jesus' resurrection, some counselees believe that their good deeds, attendance in church, and other practices result in salvation. The essence of Calvary and the atonement of Jesus' blood cannot be grasped through the deeds of the flesh. Another look at Simon the sorcerer illustrates this point. Simon believed and was baptized, but he still needed the Holy Ghost.[112] It is within the counseling setting that many counselees face the reality that they have had a form of God with no power. Therefore, the counseling session can be the introduction to the power necessary to overcome sin. Many, like Simon, need to grow deeper into the things of God. Some people verbalize their belief in Christ and His ability to forgive sin but may not have adopted the *kingdom culture*. The kingdom culture is based on the kingdom of God. Jesus described the kingdom like a mustard seed, which a man took and planted in his garden.[113] The seed grew and became a tree. He further compared it to yeast that a woman took and mixed into about sixty pounds of flour until it permeated every part of the dough[114]. Why is it necessary to adopt the kingdom culture? The kingdom principle shared by Jesus is based on growth and an expanding knowledge of Him. As one's knowledge of God expands, the goodness and delivering power of God is not only evident but is also able to be fully experienced by the counselee.

Ed Welch shared his experience counseling the Christian wife of a man who was said to be an atheist. Welch reported that he was sought out by the man for counseling on the behalf of his wife because he knew that she would possibly receive the help if the counselor was a Christian.[115] The husband attended sessions with his wife and sat on the other side of the room while the wife received counseling. Welch talked about how over time the husband would engage in the counseling, encouraging the wife to trust Jesus and to listen to Him. Eventually, the husband came to the crossroad of faith and unbelief, leading him to seek out Welch for his *own* personal counseling benefit. The "once unbelieving" husband not only confessed how he was drawn by the counseling and the help his wife had received, but he, himself, also wanted a relationship with Jesus. He confessed that the sessions were more beneficial to him than he had imagined they would be to his wife. Welch contrasted this example with another experience with a friend who was atheist. Welch's friend solicited help with his wife on one occasion and with his daughter a year to follow. Welch would meet and pray with his friend to encourage him in ways that he could serve both his wife and his daughter during each of their times of need. When Welch offered him to talk more about Jesus, the friend declined to do so. Christian counselors should remain open to the will of God in every situation and at every stage. In 1 Corinthians 3:6 (KJV) Paul says, "I have planted, Apollos watered; but God gave the increase."[116] Counseling efforts should not be cancelled or refuted for fear that the expected outcomes will not come to fruition. The Christian counselor should continue counseling with confidence in God in every situation no matter the outcome. Perhaps in the case of Welch's last example, someone *else* will be able to reach his friend with the Word of God.

Grace in Counseling

Just as grace is received, grace should be given. Think about that for a moment. Christians are supposed to and should possess the character of God. God is gracious in His dealing with mankind. The Word of God states that the Lord longs to be gracious toward us and, therefore, will rise up to show compassion.[117] The Word establishes that not because of anything we have done have we been saved. It is the grace which has been given to us in Christ Jesus before the beginning of time.[118] God's intention all along has been that we would dwell with Him. The Christian offering counsel should embrace his or her role as an opportunity to be of service to God and someone else in need. The counselor must not forget that Christ died for "whosoever," meaning both him or her (the counselor) and the counselee. There is a common denominator existing among all mankind at birth and that denominator is sin. Romans 3:23–24 is clear that all have sinned and come short of the glory of God.[119] Freely, by grace through redemption, we are all justified. The counselor should not see himself or herself as having arrived or better than the counselee. Superiority in counseling belongs to the Holy Spirit. It must be understood that a healthy counselor-counselee relationship is a vital part of reaching successful results. The conversion of the unbeliever may take several sessions. Patience is highly encouraged. Much emphasis on extending the ministry of grace and the need to forgive and be forgiven is important. Grace should not be understood by the counselee as a "safety-net" or "voucher" for sinning. Instead, grace should be presented as a *means* to experiencing the redemptive power of God. The counselee should be encouraged to believe and receive God for His work on Calvary and not simply for his desired counseling outcomes. Oftentimes, the desired outcome will not manifest, especially if it does not align with the will of God. During the course of counseling, the counselee's perspective may change as the counseling becomes effective and understandable. Consider Paul in 2 Corinthians 12:8–9. He had pleaded with the Lord three times to remove a "thorn" from his flesh.[120] The Lord denied Paul's request. Herein lies the perfect example of what it means to trust and depend on God. Paul had seen great miracles, and many of those miracles God chose to perform through Paul. God assured Paul that His grace is sufficient and that His power or His strength is made perfect in weakness. The counselee who has an understanding of this grace will learn dependency on God. Otherwise, the counselee risks the tragedy of becoming self-dependent rather than attributing glory to God. The counselee can learn from Paul's example that it is right to still trust God when one's personal desire is not met. It is inadvisable to mislead unbelievers to believing in God based upon his or her desire to have a need met. I witnessed this several times on the mission field. In some cases, missionaries would challenge the people in need to accept their religion and the result would be food, shelter, clothing, or some other item known to be scarce in exchange. Oftentimes, people want to see a sign before they will believe God. It cannot be denied that many have and will accept Jesus as Lord of their lives because of signs, wonders, and miracles. However, salvation should not be presented as a gamble. The counselor and the counselee do not control the outcomes. Both must be willing to submit to the power and the authority of the Holy Spirit even when their preferred outcome is not manifested. Considering the thorn in his flesh, Paul did not decide to reject God after He answered Him contrary to his desire. The counselee should view and receive God in the light of who He is and not based on what He can do only. Any decision to trust God based solely on what He can do compromises the integrity of counseling and is no different from the practice of witchcraft. Shadrach, Meshach, and Abednego, three Jews in captivity, were facing a fiery furnace for their refusal to abide by King Nebuchadnezzar's decree to bow to his golden statue.[121]

These three owned their faith in the face of adversity. True believers will own their faith when faced with tough situations. When the intensity of a situation heightens, the counselor should encourage the counselee to possess the same faith –faith under fire– as Shadrach, Meshach, and Abednego. Of course, they did not want to suffer or be destroyed in the fiery furnace. They chose to face their adversary with the confession of faith that God was able to deliver them and that if He did not do so they would not reject God to worship other gods. This passage is a great reference source for teaching the counselee the importance of steadfastness and how to accept the will of God. The three Jewish lads believed that God knew what was best for them. The counselee must also believe God knows what is best and stay the course when the anticipated outcome doesn't manifest.

CHAPTER 5

COUNSELING WITHOUT COMPROMISING CHRISTIAN BELIEFS AND WITHOUT CONDEMNATION TOWARD THE COUNSELEE

Effective *Christian* counseling requires adherence to the Word of God. No generic solution will work in this setting. Unlike other counselors, therapists, psychologists, and psychiatrists who may be given over to their own preference for caring for clients and patients, the Christian counselor cannot adhere to other alternatives without the risk of compromise. Other forms of help for the counselee may be influenced by the opinion of the counselor as the person providing the therapy or help. Therefore, caution should be taken when choosing a Christian counselor. A Christian seeking the help of a Christian counselor should ask questions regarding the tools and methods used in sessions. Unfortunately, there are counselors posing under the heading of a "Christian counselor" who practice according to their *personal* biases. The problem is that the personal biases of the counselor may not be congruent with the Word of God, often leaving the counseling void of grace and empathy. It is not within the role of the counselor to determine what is right or wrong necessarily. The Word of God is the authority, and the Holy Spirit is the leader in this regard. A Christian counselor who is not totally submitted to the Word of God poses a great threat to the integrity of counseling.

John 3:17

John 3:16 reveals the intense, intentional love of God for anybody and everybody. Reconciliation, restoration, atonement, and grace are apparent messages in the purposeful portrait of Calvary, but love is the framework. Love is the motivating factor which led God to carry out the mission on Calvary. John 3:16 is one of the most quoted scriptures of the Bible because it reveals the all-encompassing love of God for creation and illustrates His selfless sacrifice. The selfless love does not end with verse 16 of John Chapter 3. Verse 17 reveals the passion of God.[122] A critical look at the passage gives proof of the purpose of Jesus' life on earth. John says that Jesus was not sent by the Father to condemn the world, but to save it instead.[123] Condemn, in the passage, means to pronounce a sentence or to judge. According to Romans 6:23, mankind should have been sentenced to death.[124] The purpose of Jesus' coming to earth is restated in John10:10. This verse confirms that Jesus came to give life and to satisfy the need for death by becoming the ultimate sacrifice.[125] John 3:16 describes the Father's heart toward the sinner. While the sinner could not have done what Jesus did in verse 16, verse 17 opens the door to allow the sinner to see an example of what he or she *can* do. This is not to suggest that the world will be saved by anyone other than Jesus Christ. Stay with me. However, He is a model of what disciples or followers can do to make a "world of difference." The message in verse 17 should motivate every believer to share the gospel with unbelievers free of condemnation. Jesus, the Son of God who is Himself God, assumes this humble position to demonstrate the role of Christians. Christians should recognize three critical points: the <u>need</u> to be saved, the <u>grace</u> to be saved, and the <u>privilege</u> to evangelize and disciple others. No one is exempt from the need to be saved. Romans 3:23 speaks explicitly to the fact that all have sinned and as a result have fallen away from God.[126] Paul taught on the exceeding riches of God's grace shown toward mankind through Christ Jesus in Ephesians Chapter 2. In verse 8, he declared that salvation is by grace through faith.[127] It is not the work of man, but the gift of God.[128] That is the grace to be saved. Jesus has a message for believers in John 14:10–13 (KJV).

> "Believest thou not that I am in the Father, and the Father in me? the words that I speak unto you I speak not of myself: but the Father that dwelleth in me, he doeth the works. Believe me that I am in the Father, and the Father in me: or else believe me for the very works' sake. Verily, verily, I say unto you, He that believeth on me, the works that I do shall he do also; and greater works than these shall he do; because I go unto my Father. And whatsoever ye shall ask in my name, that will I do, that the Father may be glorified in the Son."

In verse 10, He shares with the disciples that He does not speak of Himself, but of the Father.[129] He also shares that He does the works of the Father. He admonishes them to believe that He is in the Father and the Father is in Him. The last part of verse 11 leads into what is the believer's responsibility.[130] Here, it is implied that Jesus is saying to believe Him for the sake of works. He invites the Christian into two special roles: evangelism and discipleship. When the "whosoever" referred to in John 3:16 becomes a believer, he or she gains a new job description which is revealed in John 14:12. Here, Jesus says he who believes on Him will do the works that He does and *greater* than these (the works Jesus had demonstrated) he (the believer) will do.[131] Hallelujah! Verse 13 says "whatsoever" the believer asks in His name He will do it that God the Father will be glorified. Don't lose sight of "whatsoever" as we continue alone here in our discussion. This is the grace for evangelizing and discipling others. This is also the grace that must be evidenced in Christian counseling. For us to win, we have first got to be won! This grace must be implemented apart from condemnation. John 14:13 makes the last part of verse 11 so powerful. Again, in verse 11, Jesus pleads with the disciples to believe that He is in the Father and that the Father is in Him for works' sake. This may seem contradictory to Ephesians 2:7–9 when Paul writes that salvation is not by works of man but is a gift of God. Well then, what does work have to do with it if man is not saved by his own works? The work that Jesus is talking about is *because of grace.* Because of grace, the "whosoever" in John 3:16 is evangelized into a believer. Once whosoever becomes a believer of Jesus Christ, he or she can ask "whatsoever." That's good news! Many people believe that "whatsoever" refers to any desire of the heart of a Christian. However, "whatsoever" refers to the desires of a heart aligned with God. God's heart is revealed in John 3:16. Jesus is letting His disciples know that He will fulfill the work of salvation. The believer need only ask in the name of Jesus, and Jesus will perform it. This resonates with John 3:17. The purpose of Jesus' life on earth in saving the world and not condemning the world is congruent with the assignment given to believers in John 14:10–13. John 3:17 says that the world through Him might be saved.[132] This phrase confirms the work is of Jesus Christ; yet He allows believers the opportunity and privilege to be partakers in the work of grace. Paul expressed this to the church at Philippi. He greeted them from a heart of love filled with gratitude. He spoke of the correctness of his heart in feeling compassion toward them and he acknowledged them for being partakers of grace with him both in his imprisonment and in the defense and confirmation of the gospel.[133] As observed here, compassion and grace are obvious companions in the scripture.

Evangelism and discipleship are the result of grace and compassion. Both are accomplished without condemnation. The Christian counselor has a great advantage in being able to evangelize and/or disciple counselees. The counselor's reliance upon the Holy

Spirit is paramount because of the greater works promise given by Jesus to His disciples. The counselor, who because of his own experience of the saving grace of God, should work as a *disciple* of Jesus Christ. Every believer is ordered by the great commission to share the gospel. Once that message is accepted, the new believer needs to be discipled into fellowship with God by training, teaching, and wise counsel from other disciples. This further supports the importance of the role of the Christian counselor. Counselees are often in need of evangelism and/or discipleship training. Counselors should always remember that the work of evangelism and discipleship is accomplished only when God is present in the work.

Another look at John 3:17 reveals that God did not send Jesus to condemn the world. Clearly, if God did not give Jesus the task of condemnation, then no Christian is assigned that task either. Condemnation is the fruitless adversary to evangelism and discipleship. *Condemnation is the fruitless adversary to evangelism and discipleship.* There is no typo here but instead intentional repetition. Counseling without condemnation does not preclude the need to speak firmly against sin. Sin can be addressed without compromise of the gospel and yet be without condemnation. Christian counselors who are passionate about the things of Christ will possess compassion for His people. Passion will lead them not to spare the Truth (His Word) and compassion will lead them to share it in love.

Paul wrote in Romans 8:1 there is now no condemnation to them which are in Christ Jesus, who walk not after the flesh but after the Spirit.[134] It is important to know who "them" are in the text. "Them" refers to those who do not live carnally, but who have decided that they will walk in accordance with the Holy Spirit's leading. To put it plainly, he is talking about Christians. This leaves room for questioning what happens with those who do not accept Jesus Christ as Lord. Since Paul does not mention them in Romans 8, is it permissible to condemn them? John 3:18 is transparent in this regard. Here it is clear that the person who does not believe, the unbeliever, is already condemned because he or she has not believed in the name of the only begotten Son of God.[135] Victory over sin is an essential goal of biblical or Christian counseling. The answer here serves two distinctions. One is that it is not permissible to condemn which is verified in verse 17. The other distinction is that the unbeliever is already condemned by not believing. Therefore, Christian counselors should agree with Dr. Jay Adams, that the need for salvation is always a priority. While Dr. Adams's stance on pre-counseling for evangelistic purpose is often criticized by some, the main focus ought to be that evangelism happens when necessary. To know that someone needs salvation and not offer it to him or her is like consenting to condemnation. Indifference in counseling is nothing short of a sin of omission.[136] For to know what is right and not do it is sin.[137]

Self-righteousness

Thomas Merton says, "Our job is to love others without stopping to inquire whether or not they are worthy. That is not our business, and in fact, it is nobody's business. What we are asked to do is love and this love itself will render both ourselves and our neighbor worthy."[138] Christians should ponder the thought, "How can I love if I am condemning?" Christians are commanded to love one another.[139] Jude implies that Christians are to have compassion on others and make a difference by snatching them out of the fire, showing mercy with fear, and hating the garment stained by flesh.[140] God loves the sinner but hates sin. By dying for all mankind, Jesus placed value on the sinner and not the sin. Therefore, believers have no righteousness of themselves.[141] Let's be clear that righteousness is of God and of Him alone. This cancels any supremacy other than God Himself.

Charles Spurgeon said that the greatest enemy to human souls is the self-righteous spirit which makes men look to themselves for salvation.[142] A critical analysis of moral relativism reveals that no absolute or universal moral standard exists in any situation where "self" is the leading authority. Self-righteousness is often justified in the minds of the self-righteous by blaming others. Imagine having a self-righteous person as a counselor. He or she may be good at identifying problems but how intentional would he or she be relative to offering solutions to those problems? Would such counselor really want the counselee to get better considering that identifying problems in the lives of others makes him or her feel justified in his or her own life? Consider the challenge of working with a *counselee* who displays self-righteous behaviors. There are some people who will be encountered in counseling who believe that everyone else is the problem. Not everybody who seeks counseling does so because they think something is wrong with them. Some are seeking validation for their self-righteous behaviors. Christian counselors must be cognizant of these behaviors, thoughts, and ideals. Often these traits exist as interwoven threads into the fabric of narcissism and arrogance.

Self-righteousness is the characteristic of one who is morally narrow-minded and sees oneself superiorly to others especially in contrast to their actions and beliefs. If these roots are not dealt with, we will see leaves bearing the bitter fruit of racism, hatred, pride, classism, and discrimination. Non-Christian counselors may attribute this character to some psychological issue that only deals with its symptoms but never uncovers its roots. Edward Welch makes the distinction between selfishness and self-righteousness by observing two extremes, license and legalism.[143] Both are a disregard for God as the authority over life. Welch describes the licentious church as one who teaches cheap grace and neglects the work of discipleship all while refusing to deny self. The licentious church is the canvas of a group of people suffering from idealistic distortion based on their own desires. If I might add, this church has itself as its standard. Churchgoers have given themselves a license or permission to determine what is right. It is important to note that what is right to some may not be righteous to God. He describes the legalistic church as crushing, overly scrupulous, compulsive versions of Christians.[144] Regarding legalistic church life, Welch says,

> "Legalistic church life is authoritarian and misguided about discipleship; it nourishes allegiance to manmade codes and standards as the proof of salvation. Legalism downplays God's grace; it exalts the desires of the flesh for self-righteous performance, perfectionism, self-atonement, and judgmentalism. The flesh opposes the gospel of God and lives to perform up to standards of human making. Imagine someone leading from either of these extremes. These two extremes possess two common distortions, self and grace. A distorted view of self which leads to haughtiness and pride is damaging for the one who sees himself this way. The distorted view of grace does not allow for one to embrace the blessing of it."[145]

What we are seeing here is the extremities often associated with behaviors and beliefs in the church. It resembles the far left and far right political jargon. Obviously, there is no place for these swaying behaviors. Welch's description of license and legalism in the church support the need for equilibrium for both the counselor and the counselee. That equilibrium is reached when both are in humble alignment with the Holy Spirit.

The need for humility for both the counselor and counselee is significant for reaching successful outcomes. The Apostle Paul says in Romans 12:3 (KJV), "For I say, through the grace given unto me, to every man that is among you, not to think *of himself* more highly than he ought to think; but to think soberly, according as God hath dealt to every man the measure of faith." (emphasis mine) He warns against high-mindedness. Self-righteous people are often intoxicated with pride, constipated with arrogance, and wreaking of criticism aimed toward others. He further admonishes as follows in Romans 12:16 (KJV), "Be of the same mind one toward another. Mind not high things, but condescend to men of low estate. Be not wise in your own conceits." The individual who thinks himself to be superior to others judges them. Self-righteous people often act under the distorted belief that they have a moral standard above others by comparing their works (legalism) to the works of others. Christian counselors for this reason must establish that Jesus Christ has lifted the moral standard and that only He [Jesus] could fulfill the law. In the broad scope of offering help to counselees, biblical counsel must be rendered without compromise. Paul told Timothy to preach the Word. Some theologians continue to recite what Paul said without yielding to acknowledge that the Word is sufficient. He told Timothy to preach in season and out of season.[146] The Christian counselor should be committed to uncompromised biblical counsel no matter what the current events, no matter the societal trends, or opinions of the day. The Word is "instant," which means it is applicable in the "now." Paul gave instructions to spread the gospel, reproving, rebuking, and exhorting uncompromisingly and compassionately with all longsuffering and teaching or doctrine.[147] Paul's instructions are balanced with love.

Unconditional Love vs. Unconditional Positive Regard

The Word of God urges that the truth be spoken in love. True spiritual maturation and unarmed truth are bred from love and obedience to Jesus Christ. The truth does not have to be damaging or brutal to classify as uncompromising. The correct application of God's Holy Word will be effective and life changing. So, what does unconditional love qualify as? Common among commentators is the consensus that unconditional love is affection void of limitations irrespective of the behaviors of an individual. Faith contenders agree that John 3:16 speaks to the unconditional love of God that He so loved the world and gave His only begotten Son to die that mankind would be able to have eternal life. For the believer, the limitless love of Jesus is proven in that He gives eternal life. His love is further proven as unconditional in that He died for mankind while, *yet* we were sinners.[148]

Who can love unconditionally? Without doubt, God loves unconditionally, and that love has been tested and proven throughout time. The question surfaces, "Does true unconditional love exist?" Love is a theme throughout the New Testament post-Calvary. Pre-Calvary, love is *commanded* in the law of Moses. Common to the law and the grace dispensation is the *commandment* to love one another. This love is without condition or circumstance. Both inferentially and candidly, the scriptures express the importance of love. The commandment is not given *to* God but is it is given *from* God to His people. Believers are to be extenders of His unconditional love. Christians are encouraged not to do anything from selfishness or empty conceit; but, instead, to allow humility of mind and high regard for one another to be more important than one's own self-interest. It is apparent that unconditional love is available to everyone.

Christian counselors not only can share with counselees regarding the unconditional love demonstrated at Calvary, but they can also model that love in counseling sessions. Uncompromising counsel can occur in the same setting where unconditional love and compassion are practiced. The practice of unconditional love has great evangelistic and discipleship value. Love leads the way for evangelism to take place. Jesus demonstrated so when He died for mankind for generations to come. God's love has always been unconditional. Jeremiah reveals the heart of God toward Israel. He told the people that the Lord loved them with an everlasting love and with His lovingkindness He had drawn them.[149] The children of Israel were constantly being chastened and loved by God. They endured the disciplining of God and were called His sons.[150] God took several occasions to couple chastisement with love for the benefit of His people. He would not allow them to be destroyed by their own sins nor by their enemies.

Unconditional Love and Secular Counseling

Can unconditional love be incorporated into secular counseling? How can God be absent and unconditional love be present? Let's explore the arguments of some secular counselors in contrast to Christian counselors. Some secular counselors argue that true unconditional love does not exist and vouch for conditional love (love based on the behavior and actions of another). Christian counselors, on the other hand, argue that unconditional love cannot be practiced in counseling apart from God. Humanistic psychologist, Carl Rogers, the founder of client-centered therapy, is known for his theory, unconditional positive regard. Unconditional positive regard is the Rogerian theory based on two instinctual urges. First, he purported that human beings have an innate urge toward socially constructive behavior, which is always present and functional at some level. Second, he subscribed to the idea that each person had a need for self-determination, the process by which a person controls his own life.[151] He purposed that the more a person's need for self-determination is respected, the more likely their innate urge to be socially constructive will take hold. Practicing unconditional positive regard, UPR, means that the counselor has a positive attitude of respect or acceptance toward the counselee regardless of his or her faults, actions, and behaviors.[152] Contrary to psychoanalysts like Sigmund Freud, Rogers and other humanists believed that human connection in therapy does not have to be rejected. Rogers emphasized the need for genuineness and the practice of UPR by the counselor. Data supports that this counselor-counselee relationship is the largest factor in the success of therapy.[153]

An important note should be made about UPR. Practicing UPR does not mean that each and every action of an individual is accepted. The person is accepted no matter the choice of actions.

The counselor's purpose in practicing UPR is to build a trusting relationship with the counselee. Trust is a vital part of counseling and therapy, which allows the counselee to feel comfortable without being judged. Rogers was quoted as saying, "When you criticize me, I intuitively dig in to defend myself, however when you accept me like I am, I suddenly am willing to change."[154] When dealing with parenting, Rogers did not believe in being a permissive parent. He supported the idea that parents should love their children unconditionally, leading to high self-esteem and confidence in oneself. He also supported that parents could disapprove of their children's actions and behaviors without completely rejecting the child.[155]

Having talked about both unconditional love and UPR, is one superior to the other in practical application? Dr. Jay Adams holds fast the claim that biblical counseling is enough. He asserts that psychology does not need to be integrated with Christian counseling for it to be effective. He believes that biblical counseling is a stand-along. Considering the similarities between unconditional love and UPR, is it possible that unconditional love is being practiced under the disguise of unconditional positive regard in the secular setting? Let's look at the similarities and differences.

Similarities

Rogers asserted that there were two instinctual urges as mentioned, socially constructive behavior and self-determination.[156] When the two are considered from a Christian perspective, their meanings are quite like the intended meaning given by humanistic psychologists. Socially constructive behavior in the biblical sense is the imperative statement by the Apostle Paul to esteem others better than one's self.[157] Esteem basically means to hold another person with high regard. In Philippians 2:5, Paul encouraged his listeners to "let this mind be in you which was also in Christ Jesus."[158]

What is "this" mind? It is the high regard or esteem for one's fellow man. Jesus certainly had this mind at Calvary as described by John 3:16. Roger also asserted that people have the need for self-determination or the right to choose one's own path. Christians would assert that this is the same as free will or moral responsibility to choose to live a righteous life rather than to live incarcerated by sin. Rogers incorporated empathy as a means of caring for another nonjudgmentally. Christian counselors would suggest the use of *compassion* in this regard. The Word of God holds that we are not consumed because of the Lord's mercies and because His compassions do not fail.[159] What Rogers refers to as unconditional positive regard is for Christians the demonstrated faithfulness of God toward mankind that produces forgiveness, mercies, and grace. Barbara McMahon, MS LMHC, Counseling for Adults, Families and Children, suggests five simple truth as affirmations to follow:

- "My child's worth is non-negotiable and does not need to be earned."
- "I approve of my child without condition, although I may not approve of all the choices my child makes."
- "I give my child permission to make mistakes and I believe in his/her ability to learn from them." *(Permission here means space or room for.)*
- "I believe in my child's ability to become who they are meant to be."
- "I am here to help, understand, and provide guidelines-not to criticize" [160]

Let us consider these five simple affirmations from a Christian or biblical account. The following are scriptures which demonstrate the unparalleled unconditional love of Jesus Christ as it relates to the five statements given by McMahon: (Note that these scriptures are added by the author and not by Barbara McMahon.)

- *"Who gave himself ransom for all, to be testified in due time."* (1 Timothy 2:6 KJV) Jesus paid a debt that He did not owe. We owed a debt we were not able to pay. Jesus considered us *worth* dying for.

- *"But God commendeth His love toward us, in that, while we were yet sinners, Christ died for us."* (Romans 5:8 KJV) God, knowing the terrible and sinful state of man, gave His life for all who will believe in Him to have life.

- *"But He giveth more grace. Wherefore he saith, God resisteth the proud, but giveth grace unto the humble."* (James 4:6 KJV) God has mercy upon His children and gives room for improvement and positive change with the leading of the Holy Spirit. His children must resort to humble submission to the Holy Spirit.

- *"I can do all things through Christ who strengtheneth me."* (Philippians 4:13 KJV) *"But by the grace of God I am what I am: and his grace which was bestowed upon me was not in vain; but I labored more abundantly than they all: yet not I, but the grace of God which was with me."* (1 Corinthians 15:10 KJV) God is not blind to who we are and yet He sees the greatest potentials in us.

- *"For God sent not his Son into the world to condemn the world; but that the world through him might be saved."* (John 3:17 KJV) God will not cast His children away.

Certainly, unconditional positive regard and unconditional love have parallels. These parallels further support Dr. Adams's claim that the Bible is a sufficient stand-alone for Christian counseling as discussed in Chapter 3.

Differences

Christian counselors should stay the course with biblical counsel, never wavering in the faith to accommodate the counselee or to meet one's own criteria. Unlike unconditional love where God does not compromise His expectations of creation, UPR theorists suggest that one "lay aside" one's personal views and values to enter the world of another person, the counselee in this case. Mr. Rogers is quoted as saying the following,

> "To be with another in this [empathetic] way means that for the time being, you lay aside your own views and values to enter another's world without prejudice. In some sense it means that you lay aside your "self"; this can only be done by persons who are secure enough in themselves that they know they will not get lost in what may turn out to be the strange or bizarre world of the other, and that they can comfortably return to their own world when they wish. Perhaps this description makes clear that being empathetic is complex, demanding, and strong – yet subtle and gentle – way of being."[161]

Unconditional love on the contrary does not require the counselor to place aside his or her own value system to gain the trust of the counselee or to have proper regard for the counselee. For the counselor who does not have a "self" which is submitted to God, this may pose a problem. However, the *Christian* counselor should have submitted "self" to the Holy Spirit. When the counselor is submitted to the guidance of the Holy Spirit, he or she should not compromise to accommodate the counselee, who may be an unbeliever. Rogers also referred to a "gullible" caring by the therapist for the client. In Christian counseling, the counselor does not have to possess a gullible sense of caring for the counselee. The Christian counselor cannot practice the truth of the God's Holy Word and be gullible simultaneously. Practicing unconditional love does not mean the counselor neither must play ignorant of the existing problem, sin, nor the accompanying circumstances. Instead, unconditional love acknowledges that love covers a multitude of faults according to 1 Peter 4:8. [162]

Testimony – Sharing Congruence

Growth occurs when individuals confront problems, struggle to master them, and struggle to develop new aspects of their skills, capacities, views about life. While some argue about what the extent of proximity and access to the therapist or counselor should be, it is often helpful for the counselor to share a testimony. Sharing testimonies, or congruence, with counselee can help to win his or her trust. Proper vulnerability can be an asset to the therapy. Successful sharing of congruence is that the counselee gains access to God and not necessarily to the counselor alone. The counselee should be able to understand the shared testimony and its resulting victory in context to the counselor's submission to God. In summation, God should get the glory. Testimonies work as motivators for the counselee to believe and trust God. The Book of Revelations says that we gain victory over the enemy by the Blood of the Lamb and the word of our testimony. [163] Others can cease to live a lie when we tell them our truth. Jesus humbled Himself to the point of death and became sin for all mankind. [164] He did not consider it a compromise for Him to live among His disciples and for them and others to have access to Him.

Love and Culture

Much can be said about love over the years, across cultures, and around the world. Valentine's Day consumer spending was estimated to reach approximately 20.7 billion U.S. dollars in the United States in 2019. [165] Love has been coined throughout the years as the universal language of the world. According to Jay Lowder, love is the universal language understood by all.[166] Although communicated in many dialects, Lowder asserts that love is never a foreign language and that it is understood by all. Is love *really* universal? Or is the *need* for love universal? Who determines what love really means?

The basis of love or its root has been argued throughout all time. Relativists would probably argue that love's roots are based on beliefs, cultures, society, or historical content. After all, the adage says beauty is said to be in the eye of the beholder, right? Psychologists who study human growth and development would probably deflect to Abraham Maslow's hierarchy of needs, a motivational theory.[167] Maslow's theory is a five-tiered model of human need, including self-actualization, esteem, love and belonging, safety needs, and physiological needs. This theory suggests a universal *need* for human beings to be loved.[168] Maslow placed love at the center of the five-tiered model. This theory suggests that all human beings need love as part of their development.

Cultural Relativism

Although the need to be loved and belong seems to be a universal thought for both secular counselors and Christian counselors, the actual definition of love and its origination are not always thought of the same. Christians believe that love is absolutely of God because God *is* love.[169] So, what is love for the unbeliever? Do unbelievers fall in love? These questions may be proposed in the debate for what love is and where it began. As stated in Chapter 2, relativism is the view that truth and falsity, right and wrong, standards of reasoning, and procedures of justification are products of differing conventions and frameworks of assessment and that their authority is confined to the context giving rise to them. Relativism is the default for the lack of consensus in most debates. If Christian counseling can serve as a place for evangelism and discipleship, then it can certainly be offered to counselees of diverse cultural backgrounds with the great possibility of being effective. True Christians believe that the Word of God is the absolute truth and moral compass. A distinction must be made here regarding the Holy Bible and the Word of God. The Holy Bible contains the Word of God. The Word of God, here, should be perceived in its literal meaning as the words of God spoken by the triune God, the Father, the Son, and the Holy Spirit. This distinction is not made to suggest that other parts of the Holy Bible should not be read or believed as written. However, for moral conduct the distinction is made.

For effective Christian counseling to take place, the counselor should be aware of the cultural background of the counselee. Culture has been known as an influencer to the way individuals think and live. Culture may even influence individual thoughts about not only how a group of people live but also how they love or if they love at all. When culture is the standard for how we should live morally, politically, or philosophically, our decisions are a result of the beliefs and the experiences responsible for shaping that culture. In philosophy, cultural relativism is the view that no culture is superior to any other, that cultural beliefs are equally valid, and truth is a relative and dependent variable of the cultural environment.[170] For non-Christian cultures, this means that love is based on the beliefs which shape that culture. The counselor is responsible to share what love is from the Christian perspective.

Love and Oneness with God

Believers in Christ Jesus hold to the truth that God is love and love cannot be described apart from God. This perspective on love is held as an absolute. Believers assert that everyone has the *need* to be loved, even those who commit evil acts void of love. Love is such an important foundation for Christian living so much that it is thematic throughout the Ten Commandments. Can love be accounted as real if two people engaged in a relationship do not believe in God? Human beings have an innate ability to love and be loved. Caution must be implemented to mention that love can be

BERYL I. COWTHRAN, PH.D.

abused and misappropriated. The very first commandment given is "Thou shall have no other gods before me."[171] God sees it necessary to give this commandment. Paul says the good that I would do, I do not do it; yet the evil, I should not do, I do.[172] Sin is always competing for man's attention. Because God loves mankind *so* (see John 3:16 KJV "For God so loved…"), there is always a competing nature with man's love for God. Referring to the first commandment, it is clear that God does not want any other gods before Him. Moses, in his farewell letter to the Israelites, exhorts them to keep the covenant principles. He told them that the Lord God is one Lord and urged them to love Him with all heart, soul, and might.[173] Paul told the church at Ephesus, there is "One Lord, one faith, one God and Father of all, who is above all, and through all, and in you all."[174] Oneness and love go hand and hand. Nothing should separate God's children from His love.[175] Jesus' purpose at Calvary was to atone for the sins of mankind or make man at one with God.[176]

If true victory will be attained in counseling, the counselor must encourage the counselee to submit to God alone. First Samuel 7:3–4 (KJV) says,

> "And Samuel spake unto all the house of Israel, saying, If ye do return unto the Lord with all your hearts, then put away the strange gods and Ashtaroth from among you, and prepare your hearts unto the Lord, and serve Him *only*: He will deliver you out of the hand of the Philistines. Then the children of Israel did put away Baalim and Ashtaroth, and served the Lord *only*." (emphasis mine)

The children of Israel were in a constant battle to remain faithful to God. As they encountered other nations, they were constantly being reminded to be loyal in heart and practice to God alone. Here in 1 Samuel 7:3–4, it is clear that they have adapted to the culture of other nations thereby pursuing the worship of other gods.

Entertaining the notion that they could worship God and the gods of the cultures around them, they were found to be engaging in pluralism. Pluralism in this context is the idea that the children of Israel could serve God and the other gods.[177] We see this very thing happening in America right now. Our "One Nation Under God" has decided to step out or cheat on God to conveniently meet our own individual desires. The children of Israel, like Americans, needed to be reminded that God is never to be treated as "one of" our gods. He is the One and only God. Scripture says no man can serve two masters; he will either hate one and love the other or hold the one and despise the other.[178]

Christian counselors should adhere absolutely to the word. Contrary to relativist theories, the Word of God is superior in counseling. Counselees should be encouraged to suspend any activities or therapies which contradict it. What about marriage to an unbeliever? Paul warned against being unequally yoked together with unbelievers.[179] Marriage should mirror the covenant between God and the church. How can the two become one? How can they walk together? Scripture says the two, man and woman, shall become one flesh and no longer two.[180] If the two are unequally yoked, is it safe to judge that God has put them together? Christian counselors must visit salvation in the pre-marital counseling setting. It should not be assumed that because one individual in the relationship is a believer that the other is also. In the case of individuals who are married to an unbeliever, the believer should advocate for the salvation of the spouse.

Kingdom Culture

The Old Testament documents many occasions when the children of Israel were influenced by the culture of nations surrounding them. The Apostle Paul worked with the Gentiles and Jews to come to common ground regarding culture and practices. Love is prioritized in his teachings. Just as the Gentiles had to put away their gods, the Jews had to put away their ritualistic and legalistic behaviors. As witnessed in the Books of Acts, the Holy Spirit used the apostles to continue building upon the kingdom culture. Paul's remarks to the mixed audience of Gentiles and Jews brought them to the place of oneness. He told them that they were no more strangers and foreigners, but fellow citizens with the saints, and of the household of God.[181] This foundation was of the apostles and prophets, but Jesus Christ himself is the chief corner stone.[182] Let's bring that home. The Jews and Gentiles both had to be willing to come to the center. That center must exist as Jesus Christ. When we all work toward the kingdom culture, we can come together in marriages, families, communities, and in religious assemblies. Political parties, racism, sexism, and classism are just a few of the cultural differences which separate us from one another. This is not the will of God. Hence, counseling that promotes the kingdom culture works toward celebrating diverseness in creation while working together for the highest good of all.

Discipleship is the manner by which the kingdom culture is constructed. When Jesus chose the twelve disciples, he taught them the kingdom of God. The exponential growth of the church is not in numbers, but in disciples. Disciples change communities. This is why it is so important that the church creates a culture beyond the walls of the buildings. The writer of Hebrews encourages believers not to neglect meeting together or fellowshipping together.[183] Fellowship contributes to a culture of like-mindedness with no divisions.[184] Christian conditioning occurs in the lives of new believers when other believers lead lives congruent with their profession of faith. Paul admonished young Timothy to be an example to all believers in word, conversation, in charity, in spirit, in faith, and in purity.[185] As new converts are discipled, the kingdom of God increases as described in Luke 13:18–21.[186]

How does this apply to counseling? Cultural relativism can lead to a misguided movement toward pluralism and the toleration of sin. A kingdom culture, on the other hand, enhances the lives of individuals who submit to the one and only God, by providing a place of victory and hope against sin. Christian counseling provides a faith community for the counselee to be surrounded by believers. The Kingdom of God is a place of growth for the believer. This is yet another supportive reason for evangelism and discipleship in counseling.

PART III

COMPASSIONATE COUNSELING WITHOUT CONDEMNATION IN THE 21ST CENTURY

CHAPTER 6

ANSWERING THE CALL AND THE QUESTION: ARE THOSE OF US WHO ARE CALLED READY TO ANSWER THE QUESTION?

Are those of us who have answered the call ready for the question? There are many questions with which pastors, teachers, evangelists, and 21st century leaders are faced with. Christian leaders are faced with difficult questions surrounding abortion, suicide, sexual orientation, murder, smoking, and the list goes on. In a morally relativistic world, it has become increasingly more difficult to confront these questions. Over the past years, there are several declining trends in church membership and religious affiliation. There is an obvious decline in trust and confidence in organized religion. Many have chosen to remain religious or spiritual without associating or gathering on a regular basis with an assembly. A 2019 Gallup poll reveals that church membership in the United States is down sharply for the past two decades.[187] On average, there has been a 17% difference in church membership when comparing the 69% of U.S. adults who were members of a church in 1998-2000 with the 52% in 2016-2018.[188] Another trend in the data reveals that an increasing trend in no religious preference is a key factor in the decline in church membership. Out of the four generational categories–Millennials, Generation X, Baby Boomers, and Traditionalists–Millennials demonstrated the lowest percentage, 42%, of its generational category's engagement in church membership in 2016-2018.[189] When Generation X was the same age as Millennials, they demonstrated 62% of their generational category who were engaged in church membership.[190] This is a 20% difference between the generations at the same age.[191] Traditionalists, born 1945 or earlier, lead the way among generations with a religious preference. Millennials, born 1980-2000, trend opposite of Traditionalists leading the way among those who have no religious preference within their generational category. The numbers in the Gallup poll also reveal that there are fewer people in each generational category who have a religious preference and who actually have a church membership as well.

Does this decrease in church membership mean there will be an increase in Christian counseling? Will we start to see an indirect correlation between church membership and counseling needs? Some would say that the decrease in church membership may lead to a *decrease* in Christian counseling as a result of them not wanting to deal with Christianity any longer. However, just because people are leaving the church, does not mean that *need* for Christian counseling will not increase. Much is to be discerned regarding the said decline in church membership. Some believe that non-denominational churchgoers, referred to as "nones," are being counted among unbelievers, when in fact, they believe in God but are not committed to any religion.[192] There are those who may have left church but contend that they have not left God. What happens to morality because of the decline in fellowship and church membership? There is much to consider. Can the decline in church membership correlate with an increasing number of crimes committed in the United States? Can the decline in church membership correlate with a decrease in morality? These are trends that certainly need to be monitored. However, there is a need for the church to train disciples and build counselors. Perhaps some people will not meet God by coming into the front door of a church building. However, that does not disqualify the possibility of someone meeting God in the counselor's office or a virtual platform. The Christian counselor should remain encouraged and endeavor even the more to train for biblical counseling in a world where moral decline is happening. Rather than to look at Christian counseling as an alternative among growing others, the church and Christian counselors should view it as the only working possibility. It should be respected as an opportunity for leading many *back* to God while leading others *to* Him.

How will the Christian counselors answer the tough questions of the day? Traditionalists, when interviewed, overall report that the times are increasingly revealing a move away from godly living. Many Traditionalists and Baby Boomers (1946-1964) report that they believe the end times are nigh. No matter the consensus or the contrary, Christian counseling must offer answers to the problems for the world today. Paul charged Timothy to study or to strive to show himself approved to God so that he could unashamedly apply the Word of Truth.[193] Christians must stand ready to defend the gospel. We must also be ready to teach the Word and answer the tough questions.

The Call

Whoever is called *upon* is called. God calls everyone to salvation. He calls everyone to believe by faith. He calls everyone to a technical work or an assignment. The assignments may vary from person to person, but the Great Commission is clear for all. God intends for every believer to make disciples. Servants of God are commanded to go into the highways, byways, and hedges with the compelling message of the gospel to urge people to come to Him.[194] Believers are called to the greater works.[195] God has saved believers and called believers with a holy calling according to His purpose and grace.[196]

Because of the grace of God, believers should be eager to serve and to draw others toward Christ. Therefore, Christians should speak with grace, seasoned with salt that they may provide Christ as the answer for every man.[197]

Jesus does not call without equipping. Christian counselors and Christian leaders should never be given to a spirit of fear when addressing issues. Jeremiah reveals an open invitation for dialogue with God. God says, "Call me and I will answer you."[198] God promises that He will answer with great and mighty things unbeknownst to the one who asks.[199] The believer must believe the unstoppable, incomprehensible, uncontainable nature of God as revealed in the name "I Am That I Am."[200] The Christian counselor, who is a believer, should embrace, the all-knowing, all-sufficient, self-existent, all-present *being* of God. When God sent Moses to do the technical work of his calling, He assured him that He is the all-sufficient God. Moses had no choice but to depend on God and to take Him at His Word. When facing Pharaoh, a Red Sea, or even an army of many, our faith must be firmly rooted in God and not in the "self" that psychologists focus on so much. The Book of Acts is often referred to as the Book of the Acts of the Apostles. Because of this title, some limit the works of miracles documented in the early church age to an earlier time. The Book of Acts is really the work of the Holy Spirit *through* the apostles. The Holy Spirit is still capable of doing the impossible and providing the answer for tough situations.

Romans Chapter 1: The Sins of Man

In Romans Chapter 1, Paul found himself addressing a group of Gentiles who had been recently converted. He had the task of sharing the universal need for righteousness which required him to tell them of their guilt. He, then, mentioned to them their call to being saints.[201] This was a call to a continued life with God filled with peace and grace.[202] Verse 18 is filled with a warning against the ungodliness and unrighteousness of men who withhold the truth, having knowledge of it.[203] This verse further supports the premise that Christian counseling should be conducted without delay or compromise of the gospel. Counselors, as believers, are commanded to share the truth or risk the wrath of God. The consequences of not adhering to biblical counsel do not apply to the counselee alone but also to the counselor. Romans Chapter 1 speaks of how men become vain in their own hearts and fail to glorify God. This further supports Dr. Jay Adam's claim that biblical counsel is enough. Dr. Adam's does not support the claim that use of psychology and other sciences are necessary to justify Christian counseling. I am not suggesting that medical care for counselees will not be warranted. Chemical imbalances and neurological disorders may require medical intervention. The need for these resources does not cancel out Christian counseling. Plausibility for Dr. Adam's claim can be supported by verse 22 which reads, "Professing themselves to be wise, they become fools."[204] Sigmund Freud's denouncement of religion is a clear rejection of God as an authority in counseling. The lack of glory attributed to God through theories "coined" by men who must observe another man outside of the lens of God in order to arrive at their conclusion, accounts for the lack of success with some counseling methods. God is Creator and need not observe His creation to know what is best. Instead, the Holy Bible serves as a manual for Christian living. Disobedience to God leads to the judicial acts of God. It is a very tragic thing for a man to believe his own lie. When man refuses to adhere to the truth of God's Word and yet live based upon his own lie, the wrath of God unfolds. In Romans Chapter 1, God allows for the disobedient to be given over to uncleanness through the lust of their own hearts, vile affections and sexual depravity, and a reprobate mind void of the principles of God.[205] These three results of disobedience have led to many of the sins which have become widely accepted during current times. The scripture identifies the resulting behaviors as fornication, wickedness, covetousness, maliciousness; full of envy, murder, debate, deceit, malignity; whisperers, backbiters, haters of God, despiteful, proud, boasters, inventors of evil things, disobedient to parents, without understanding, covenant breakers, without natural affection, implacable, unmerciful: who knowing the judgment of God, that they which commit such things which are worthy of death.[206] These *behaviors*, as psychologist would refer to them, are *sins* according to the Bible. God deals with sin. The work of the Christian counselor is to help counselees identify sin in their lives and to assist them with seeing the need for righteousness.

A Parallel Examination of Sin in 2 Timothy 3

Paul's first candid address of unrighteous living in Romans Chapter 1 was not his last. Excluding speculation of who the author of Hebrews is, 2 Timothy is the last of the Pauline epistles. In this final letter, he encourages young Timothy to continue in the work with excitement and without fear. Paul's encouragement of Timothy sounds similar to his own confession in Romans Chapter 1. In Verse 16, Paul made the proclamation that he was not ashamed of the gospel of Christ.[207] He recognized the gospel as the power of God unto salvation to everyone who believes. By the time he wrote the Book of 2 Timothy, Paul had a robust assurance of his prior conviction in Romans 1:16. In 2 Timothy 1:8, he encouraged Timothy not to be ashamed of the testimony of Jesus, nor of Paul himself, a prisoner.[208] He further urges Timothy to be a partaker of the afflictions of the gospel according to the power of God. The parallels in these Pauline writings are not to be ashamed of the gospel and that the gospel is the power of God. Believers can conclude from these writings that it is important to unashamedly proclaim the gospel of Jesus Christ. Believers can also presume that the power of the gospel is irreplicable. Paul further asserted his unapologetic claim of the gospel and his persuasion of the assurance of salvation in 1 Timothy 1:12.[209] Another parallel exists between Romans 1:29 and 2 Timothy 2:16. Paul warned against debate and deceit and urged Timothy to shun profane and vain babblings or disputes.[210] Christians must not waste time with such. Unbelievers spend energy on disproving the Word, but never proving their own stance. Christian counselors need only teach the truth of God's Word without debate.

In Paul's warning of the coming apostasy and perilous times, he told Timothy to expect things that he formerly warned the Gentiles about in Romans Chapter 1. The Apostle warned that men shall be lovers of their own "selves."[211] It is worth it to note here that many of the psychology claims and theories give credence to this as evidenced by their focus on "self." Hence, it can be observed that morality is often based on what the individual desires it to be according to "self." He further warned that men would be covetous, boasters, proud, blasphemers, disobedient to parents, unthankful, unholy, without natural affection, truce breakers, false accusers, incontinent, fierce, despisers of those that are good, traitors, heady, high-minded, lovers of pleasures more than lovers of God, having a form of godliness with no power. Paul warned that these men would always learn but never arrive at the knowledge of truth. As in Romans 1:28, Paul resolved in 2 Timothy 3:8, that such men would be given over to a reprobate or unprincipled mind.[212] Nevertheless, he still encouraged Timothy in the Word stating that all scripture is given by inspiration of God, and is useful for teaching, reproving, and correction for instruction in righteousness. This admonition further supports the claim that the scripture is sufficient for counseling.

The charge to Timothy is one that Christian leaders and counselors must receive as admonishment to uncompromisingly adhere to the Word of God. Imperatively and passionately, Paul charged Timothy to preach the word and to be instant in season and out of season.[213] He charged him to reprove, rebuke, and exhort with all longsuffering and doctrine.[214] This charge is one that is traditionally given to pastors and preachers of the gospel. However, the Christian counselor can also embrace the challenge to reprove, rebuke, and exhort with love the counselee. Uncompromised love in the delivery of counseling techniques leads the way for success in counseling.

The Need for Doctrinal Teaching: Sanctification and Justification

Christian counselors are faced with providing an answer for the long list of sins and behaviors that lead to separation from God and the need for counseling. In the letter to the church at Corinth, Paul raises a question. This question is actually a *statement* in interrogative form, which says that the unrighteous will not inherit the kingdom of God. He lists many of sins which are listed in Romans Chapter 1 and 2 Timothy Chapter 3. In 1 Corinthians 6:9–11, Paul addresses the need for sanctification and justification. Here, he provides an answer to the sins and behaviors that cause a separation from God. Have we neglected to teach these foundational principles as essentials for salvation? When a professing Christian cannot define these essentials to salvation, a deeper assessment of one's relationship with God is necessary. Often, people need ongoing Christian education. Nearly every profession requires recertifications, licensing, and/or continuing education hours. While we as Christians may not have to recertify our salvation, we are called to repent and to study to show ourselves approved unto God. It is important that the local church educate members and the community on the essentials for salvation.

Sanctification

John 17:17 (KJV) says, "Sanctify them through thy truth: thy word is truth." How will change occur for any of us? We must receive the truth of the inerrant Word of God for change to occur. The Word works sanctification by setting us apart to be used of

God. Sanctification is the consistent work of God's grace in the life of believers. Jesus demonstrates sanctification in His life on earth. He came into the world; yet; He lived a life set aside unto the Father. While *salvation* is of paramount importance, the need for *sanctification* is necessary for "growth." Let's take a closer look at this. Salvation is like being born while sanctification represents the growth cycle beyond one's state of being at birth. When we discuss salvation, we talk about being "born again." Remember "Nick at Night," Nicodemus? Nicodemus speaks with Jesus in John Chapter 3 about the marvelous works He performs. Notice that Nicodemus acknowledges Jesus as Rabbi and he acknowledges His *works*.[215] Yet Jesus, responds to Nicodemus's inquiry with the need to be born again. We can deduce here that the works of miracles are for those who have yielded their lives to Jesus and are born again. Jesus' response is with great intention. He wants Nicodemus to focus on Him rather than on the outcomes. Often, we are more concerned about outcomes, rather than focusing on the One who controls them. We are not what we function as, but we are what we believe. We will discuss *function* in Chapter 11. Jesus wants Nicodemus to know what difference between what is authentic (what we believe) and what is artificial (what we do apart from what we believe). An authentic relationship with Jesus requires that we be born again. Many people want to do the work and experience the miracles without submitting to God and being born again. When Jesus responded, Nicodemus further inquired if he would have to enter once again into his mother's womb.[216] We must understand that the kingdom of God is inside of the believer.[217] In order for the kingdom to grow and expand, we, as believers, must grow. Take a real plant and an artificial one. We know that the real plant is authentic in nature as we witness its growth and requirement of certain things like water and light. The artificial plant, on the contrary, does not require these things and will be okay in darkness. Although it appears okay in the darkness, it will not bear growth! As mentioned before, the kingdom of God is like a seed that when planted produces its harvest.

Therefore, the ongoing process of sanctification beyond salvation is a vital part of living for God and growing in Him. Sanctification is the key factor for inheriting or possessing the kingdom of God. When we allow for the work of the Holy Spirit in our lives, the process of sanctification will become evident. This process is much like the process of photosynthesis to a plant. Now let's view this in a counseling perspective. Often counselees will admit to having *confessed* Jesus as Savior. However, the counselor must delve deeper to understand the depth of surrender the counselee has toward living for God. Jesus did not want Nicodemus to just be able to say that he had a conversation with Him at night. He wanted him to be able to have an ongoing relationship with Him in the Light! So many counselees and Christians have a conversation with Jesus in their "night season," which is often characterized by depression, anxiety, sin, or some malady. What about knowing Christ beyond the crisis? That is the need for sanctification. 1 Thessalonians 5:23 (KJV) says, "And the very God of peace sanctify you wholly; [I pray God] your whole spirit and soul and body be preserved blameless unto the coming of our Lord Jesus Christ." Here, sanctification is a *progressive* work taking place gradually and comparable to a seed sprouting to a harvest overtime. Again, the expansion of the kingdom of God is in direct correlation with the sanctification process of its inhabitants. Consequently, Christian counseling without compromise of the gospel contributes greatly to the growth of the kingdom. Where sanctification is continually at work, sin is less frequently so. So that this process continues to produce a God-intended harvest in believers, it is important to caution counselees not to abuse the gift of grace. Many accept Christ; yet abuse grace thinking that it will serve as means for excusing sin.[218] Pastors and counselors must not only encourage Christians and counselees to repent by confession of the mouth, but also in the framework of their behaviors as the process of sanctification works for a greater good.

David Powlison encourages that everyone asks themselves what God's will is for them personally.[219] He purposes the answer is clear in Paul's message to the church at Thessalonica. First Thessalonians 4:3–9 (KJV) says,

> "For this is the will of God, even your sanctification, that ye should abstain from fornication: That every one of you should know how to possess his vessel in sanctification and honour; Not in the lust of concupiscence, even as the Gentiles which know not God: That no man go beyond and defraud his brother in any matter: because that the LORD is the avenger of all such, as we also have forewarned you and testified. For God hath not called us unto uncleanness, but unto holiness. He therefore that despiseth, despiseth not man, but God, who hath also given unto us his Holy Spirit. But as touching brotherly love ye need not that I write unto you: for ye yourselves are taught of God to love one another."

It is obvious here that our sanctification is the will of God for our lives. Powlison discusses the need for sexual purity, proper regard for money, and proper human interaction and regard.[220] He lists these as part of our *daily* sanctification. He speaks of money-love as a metastasizing cancer.[221] He says that the tongue must be tempered so that we do not wreck the lives of others. Ultimately, God wants our lives to daily reflect who we are in Him. Counselees must be encouraged to continue the daily walk with Christ beyond the scope of counseling. Christians must be encouraged to continue the daily walk with Christ beyond a worship service or prayer meeting. Paul says daily we should give our bodies as living sacrifices, holy, and acceptable unto the Lord.[222] This is the work of sanctification.

Justification

While sanctification is a continual work of God in the life of the believer, justification is the action which seals the deal. Justification happens immediately. When a man has faith to believe unto salvation, he is justified by that faith.[223] The key is faith. A strong case can be made for faith through-out the scripture. The just shall live by faith.[224] *Who are the just?* Those who have been justified because they have believed are counted as the just. What does it mean to live by faith? A misconception is that this means that one can have faith *for* something and receive it. That is not the meaning here. "The just shall live by faith" is a statement which means *because* of faith, the just can live. In other words, having faith has justified the sinner and given him or her peace with God through Jesus Christ.[225] Otherwise, the sinner would remain unreconciled to God and be destined for death. Justification, simplified, is a legal term that means Jesus Christ supplied justice to the unjust and made him or her *just!* The role of faith is so important. It is the only requirement of the believer for justification. Justification is not conditional based upon the believer's works. Instead, it is like the bodyguard to sanctification in that it is always there guarding the salvation of the believer while sanctification continues its work in saving *progressively.* One must be willing to humbly and sweetly be saved. So, what does this mean? This means that one is willing to let go of any pride and allow for the work of faith. The proud man believes he can work his way into salvation, but the humble man realizes that his righteousness is because of faith in Jesus, God.[226] Pride only results in a righteousness which is of "self." This type of righteousness, self-righteousness, has "works" and "deeds" attached to it. If man's salvation was justified by works, then there would be no appreciation for the saving grace of God.

Justification is witnessed in the Bible as early as the book of Genesis. Abram believed the Lord and it was counted as righteousness for him.[227] The parallel to the Old Testament mention of this "imputed righteousness" is written about in Romans Chapter 4.[228] First, allow me to note that imputed righteousness is distinguishable from imparted righteousness. Imputed righteousness means that

God places His *own* righteousness *in* the believer as if it were his or hers to begin with. Imparted righteousness would be likened unto Joseph's coat of many colors. It would serve as a symbol worn by the owner but never becoming a part of the owner. Righteousness is not something that the believer wears like a garment. Instead, it is what continues to develop and grow inside of the believer like an interwoven fabric as sanctification is progressively at work. Second, this imputed righteousness is the key to inheriting the kingdom of God. The Word of God states that only the righteous will inherit the kingdom. It would be impossible for this to happen without the work of justification and sanctification. Without the imputed righteousness of God, there would be none who are righteous.

The Law or the Lord

The Apostle Paul in his Epistle to the churches at Galatia revisited the subject of Abraham's justification by faith. This is such a persistent theme because of its importance to the *future* of the believer. Paul gets down to business in Galatians Chapter 3. Here, he strongly admonishes the Galatians about the truth surrounding justification. Although a legal term, justification of the believer is the work of grace because of faith in Jesus Christ. The Galatians were still believing in the "psychology of the law." In modern ages, those who seek the help of psychologist as opposed to biblical counseling are subject to the laws of psychology as *theoretically* interpreted by man. Let me interject here that there is nothing theoretical about faith. This is why faith in God produces miracles. Many of the laws of psychology and the associated theories deal with "self." When getting counselees to look within and assume responsibility for their actions, the work of the psychologist may seem beneficial in getting them to check the inward perspective. However, the work is still incomplete in cases where salvation and discipleship are absent or critically needed.

The legalistic thinking of the Galatians attributed justification to the law. It may be necessary to review or think back to our previous discussions of "self" in Chapter 2 beneath the *Meta-ethical Moral Relativism* heading and in Chapter 5 beneath the heading of *Self-righteousness*. Let's continue. Paul is clear that the believer must be found in Jesus, not having his own righteousness, which is of the law; but having that which is through faith in Christ.[229] In Galatians Chapter 3, Paul talks about the work of the Holy Spirit as opposed to the independent work of man to satisfy the requirement of the law. This supports the need for the Holy Spirit in counseling. He, Paul, further notes that those who are of faith are the children of Abraham. This is important in the restoration and reconciliation of the children of faith back to God and His promises. The promise was given to Abraham and, as a result, the promise is given to the children of God. So many Christians confine this promise to material wealth alone. This promise is really embedded in the imputed righteousness which was given to Abraham. Remember the difference between imputed and imparted righteousness? Recall here that imputed righteousness means that God places His own righteousness upon believers as if it were ours from the beginning. Now, understand that those who believe by faith are also *heirs* to the promise.[230] This heirship suggests that something was placed in us by the owner of it. God imputed righteousness to Father Abraham. Look at Galatians 3:29 (KJV), "And if ye be Christ's, then are ye Abraham's seed, and heirs according to the promise." Let's talk about "Nick at Night" again. Again, Jesus wanted him to have more than just an occasion or encounter with Him. He wanted Nicodemus to have a relationship which fosters ownership. When we belong to God what belongs to God belongs to us! That's real victory. Let us review Galatians 3:29 again. It stated that if you belong to Christ, then you are a seed of Abraham. Therefore, the promise, which belongs to Abraham, also belongs to you. It is clearly undeniable that God, in His infinite wisdom, covers all bases. This is evident in that the law was fulfilled by Jesus, and that He is the end of the law so that everyone who believes may have righteousness.[231] Legalistically, the requirement for being an heir would constitute that one be proven akin to the one who held the deed or the promise. Jesus, who is God, fulfilled the requirement. God had already justified Abraham through faith and Jesus justifies believers who through faith believe in Him. Abraham, known as the father of justification, is now the father of all who are justified; thereby, making them all heirs of the promise because of Jesus Christ. Hallelujah!

The work of justification is not of man but of God and Him alone. Therefore, the law has been satisfied by Jesus and will *never* need to be satisfied again. Man need only believe upon Jesus Christ that the works He has already performed are complete and not wanting. Please comprehend that these finished works are yet still working for us today through the processes of justification and sanctification. Paul summarizes these processes in Ephesians 2:8–9 (KJV), "For *by grace* are ye *saved through faith*; and that *not of yourselves*; it is the *gift* of God; *not of works*; lest any man should boast." (emphasis mine) Let's look more intricately at the areas of emphasis I have noted in these verses. *"By grace"* means that Jesus performed this blessing not because of man's merit but because of unmerited favor. *"Saved through faith"* means that without faith it is impossible to please Him, and we cannot believe Him apart from faith. *"Not of yourselves"* expresses that glory cannot be attributed to "self." Many secular counselors rely upon self-help guides and suggest looking within for the answer. This only makes morality relative to one's self or culture. *"Gift"* means that it is given freely. When we talk about the gift, let us recall John 3:16 and how God loved the world so much that He *gave* His only begotten Son. Romans 5:8 (KJV) says, "But God commendeth his love toward us, in that, while we were yet sinners, Christ died for us." Before we can ask for anything, it is already available.[232] *"Not of works"* means that we cannot work *for* it. We work *because* of it. The work is already done, and nothing can come after the finished work of Calvary.[233]

Jesus' work on Calvary has proven to be complete. Therefore, whosoever believes in Jesus can be made whole. Relative to counseling, the Word of God is complete and can stand alone when there is implementation of a strategic plan for proper application to one's daily life. Counseling, which supports the ideas of moral relativism, will always leave the counselee battling with self-righteousness. Relativism is the issue here. Often self-righteousness is difficult to identify in the counselee because it is thought of most often to be synonymous with arrogance and shrewd behavior. Those who have not consented to the grace of God by having faith in Jesus will find themselves subjected to their own limitations. Only Jesus can liberate and release us from the chains of our own sins or problems.

Christian counselors who incorporate assessment tools that evaluate the need for salvation and the need for discipleship will be able to fulfill the *calling* of the vocation. It is not safe to assume that every counselor is fulfilling the calling to counsel. Some are just professionals performing daily duties according to textbooks and guidelines created outside of the biblical scope. These counselors rarely, if at all, participate in the process of sanctification through discipleship. The success of counseling increases when both the counselor and counselee recognize the need for the Holy Spirit. If counselees are saved, they will have had some experience with the Holy Spirit's work. Counselors should stress the need for building a relationship with the Holy Spirit as a person and not as an "it." He, the Holy Spirit, should be personified in all our lives. Such relationship will provide the counselee *someone* to consult daily, not just occasionally, regarding his or her moral choices. Otherwise, the continual work of sanctification will be hindered.

I want to be clear that I am not suggesting that counselors do not need be learned regarding theories or laws of psychology. However, they must be armed with the Word of God. This delicate balance promotes successful counseling when achievable. Also, a distinction is due to be made here; counselors should be reminded that biblical counseling outcomes are not based on the knowledge of theories, concepts, nor the ability to quote scriptures. Instead, counseling through the tough things requires that counselors build strategic methods based upon the foundational principles of the Word of God. The sins mentioned earlier in our parallel review of Romans Chapter 1 and 2 Timothy Chapter 3 should not be treated like a recurring virus for which counseling is used to treat the symptoms, but never addresses the root cause.

No matter where counselees are in their walk with the Lord, *biblical* counseling serves as a great compass. Counselees who are coming to know Christ for the first time should be given the plan of salvation and discipled upon their acceptance of Jesus as Lord. Discipline is better maintained when one has been properly and consistently discipled. For those who have lost their way, the counselor should ascertain their knowledge of the foundational principles and doctrine. Often these individuals require teaching on the doctrine of sanctification. Many believers have not received teaching about the doctrines. Most have believed based on some motivational speech, sermon, or presentation. For those who are seemingly hopeless and helpless, learning about justification will expose them to better through Jesus Christ.

The focus of the those called to Christian counseling should not be how to answer the tough questions. The focus should be on answering the call by following the lead of the One who calls. Counselors should never neglect to study and be knowledgeable of opposing thoughts regarding counseling, culture, religion, and doctrines. Intentionally, they should always depend on the Holy Spirit by adhering to His leading without compromise.

CHAPTER 7

COUNSELING IN THE 21ST CENTURY

Answering the call to ministry and/or counseling is no small commitment and should not be taken casually. Both require preparation and consistent prayer. Biblical or Christian counseling in the 21st century is necessary now more than ever. The Word of God is tried and true, having endured trials, tests, and temptations. While times certainly have changed, the Word of God remains consistent and settled. God, Himself, is consistently good, well-able, merciful, and faithful toward His creation. In an ever evolving and everchanging world, He remains consistently the same throughout all times.[234] His enduring love is the foundation upon which true Christian works are built and executed. Love must be the foundational principle guiding believers as we carry out our daily living whether it be within personal or professional settings. We will talk more about "love" in Chapter 8. For the sake of discussion here, I want to be clear that love must be the leading force in counseling if the process will be executed with uncompromising compassion. Since this is the case, the Bible must be the instructional guide for Christian leaders and counselors to draw from. If counselees are going to be guided in living their "best life," the Word of God must be respected by both counselors and counselees as the authority and standard for living.

What makes the Word of God the authority in counseling? Why

is the Word sufficient? There are numerous reasons in favor of the sufficiency and authority of the Word. One of those reasons is that the Word is settled and firmly fixed forever.[235] On the contrary, books and speculative accounts written by man regarding the meaning of real occurrences do not provide the consistency that the Bible continues to provide throughout all ages. In contrast, books written by men are in constant revision while the Word of God remains the same. One of the main goals of Christian counseling is to promote consistent righteous living. Since this is a goal of Christian counseling, why not choose a consistent source for foundational purposes? Again, God's Word is tried and true. He is faithful to His Word and watches over it to perform it (His Word).[236] What about books and theories written by man? While some of them provide great guidance counseling, it is not plausible to say that God is watching over those books and theories to perform them. But, for sure, He is watching over His word.

Because the Word is settled forever, it is the most reliable source. It is upon its foundational principles that are all other plausible *re*sources built. While some may grapple with present-day issues associated with the problem of sin, *Christian* counselors answering the call of 21ˢᵗ century counseling should not embrace the fear of not being able to find answers. While these present-day issues may be hot topics or new things for some of us to deal with, there is nothing new under the sun nor *to the Son*, Jesus.[237] Those who are called to this work should place total trust in Him. Since we are talking about the foundation of counseling, let us look at Jesus as the Chief Cornerstone. Ephesians 2:18–22 (KJV) says,

> "For through him we both have access by one
> Spirit unto the Father. Now therefore ye are no
> more strangers and foreigners, but fellow citizens
> with the saint, and of the household of God; And
> are built upon the *foundation* of the apostles and
> prophets, *Jesus Christ himself being the chief corner*

stone; In whom all the building *fitly framed together*
groweth unto an holy temple in the Lord: In whom
ye also are builded together for an habitation of God
through the Spirit." (emphasis mine)

It is clear from this passage that Jesus Christ is the solid rock of
Christianity. Therefore, His Word is independent of anything else.
Now this does not mean that other books and tools are excluded
from counseling. However, these tools are more likely to help when
they are based upon the Word. Some argue that religion should be
avoided in professional counseling making it difficult for Christian
counselors, those who use the Bible as the basis for counseling,
to be licensed. Counselors who are determined to operate within
the framework of God's Word should not despair because of the
rejection of this world. Jesus encourages that we work beyond the
rejection of man in Matthew 21:42–43 (KJV),

"Jesus saith unto them, 'Did ye never read in the
scriptures, The stone which the builders rejected,
the same is become the head of the corner: this is
the Lord's doing and it is marvellous in our eyes?
Therefor say I unto you, The kingdom of God shall
be taken from you, and given to a nation bringing
forth the fruits thereof.'"

Let me call your attention back to Chapter 6 where we discussed that
the kingdom of God is inside of the believer and it is like a seed that
when planted produces a *harvest*. Now compare this with Matthew
21:43 where is says that the kingdom of God will be taken away
from those who reject the Chief Cornerstone, Jesus, and given to
a nation that brings forth the fruit *thereof*. I want to emphasize not
only the word *fruit* but also the word *thereof*. Chapter 6 brings to light
the work of sanctification in producing the harvest of the kingdom
of God through the believer. This is so relevant to our discussion

here because Jesus is telling us in verse 43 that fruit, harvest, is an important part of His kingdom. Now, note that the word *thereof* is not just dangling there like some extra in a movie or music video. This seemingly casual word is of paramount importance to the verse. It refers to the *type* of fruit. Stay with me for this point of clarity. Non-Christians or unbelievers can produce fruit. However, one must inspect the produce! Is that fruit the fruit of the kingdom of God? Jesus urges that we produce the fruit of His kingdom! That means He must be at the center of it all if victory is going to be the fruit of counseling. Let us connect the dots. In Chapter 6, we declared that whatever belongs to God belongs to His heirs. That means that believers, who are the righteousness of God, must live in and operate from a place of victory in Christ Jesus. In Psalm 11:1–3 (NKJV) says,

> "In the Lord I put my trust; How can you say to my soul, 'Flee as a bird to your mountain'? For look! The wicked bend their bow. They make ready their arrow on the string, That they may shoot secretly at the upright in heart. *If the foundations are destroyed, What can the righteous do?*" (emphasis mine)

When kingdoms fall, philosophy fails, and earthly rulers no longer rule, Jesus remains! The victory was accomplished at Calvary where Jesus demonstrated love (the foundation) according to John 3:16. There at the Cross, He gained the victory and gave it to believers. When Jesus is invited into the counseling session, He bridges any gaps between solution and problem or counselor and counselee. Let's view it from an architectural perspective. Builders and architectural engineers can prove that the head or chief cornerstone is purposely placed at the joining of two walls to keep the building together and to prevent it from falling apart. When both the counselor and the counselee approach counseling with an open heart toward God, faith-based solutions can be built based upon the foundational love of God. I John 4: 7–10 (KJV) says,

> "Beloved, let us love one another: for love is of God; and every one that loveth is born of God, and knoweth God. He that loveth not knoweth not God; for God is love. In this was manifested the love of God toward us, because that God sent his only begotten Son into the world, that we might live through him. Herein is love, not that we loved God, but that he loved us, and sent his Son to be the propitiation for our sins."

This passage states that God is love. We have discussed that love is the foundation; therefore, God, Jesus, is the foundation for counseling. It becomes clearer why Satan wants to distort our view of love and destroy it by tampering with the institution of marriage. Fret not. Satan cannot destroy Jesus. Where Jesus, God, is the foundational basis, Satan has no power. However, he will do anything to distract believers from experiencing the length, breadth, and width of God's love. Let us consider "whosoever" again. "Whosoever" means any and everybody no matter what sin they have committed. If "whosoever" believes in Jesus, he or she can have everlasting life. Satan hates this truth. The expression of God's love was witnessed at Calvary, but its measure is yet to be fully experienced. We cannot fully explain or comprehend the love of God and His sacrifice for all who will receive Him.

Let's take a deeper look at the challenges of counseling in the 21st century. As with any other time in history, such counseling should be delivered uncompromisingly and compassionately to promote spiritual growth. Growth happens when the inner man, not "self," is strengthened. Allow me to make a distinction between the inner man and "self." Strengthening "self" can result in unhealthy behaviors leading to self-righteousness and fulfilling one's self-will. The inner man is the *being* who allows the Spirit to lead. Ultimately, Jesus wants free reign in the heart of the believer. In counseling, counselees must be willing to allow Jesus to "be at home" in their hearts. He wants to fill every bit of the believer's life. Paul taught the church at Corinth that as believers, we do not belong to ourselves because the body of the believer is the temple of the Holy Ghost.[238] God loves His children and wants to dwell in them, working sanctification and strengthening the inner man. When the inner man is strengthened, the believer can successfully live the Christian life.[239] This inner growth because of Jesus' presence within expands one's capacity and comprehension for living in the fullness of God's will. When the love of God grows within, the counselee discovers the reach to love others from that same place within. That reach extends from the limitless love of Jesus Christ.

How does this translate to Christian counseling? In the pre-evaluative phase, counselors should assess for any distorted views of love. In Chapter 2, we talked about idealistic distortion versus reality. Because Satan knows the power of love that defeated him at Calvary, he will do anything to distort or destroy the counselor's or the counselee's perspective of love. His goal is to discredit the need for true love as defined by God. Christian counselors must be conscious not to lend themselves to the work of Satan by ignoring findings in the pre-evaluative phase. He desires for counselors to extract God from counseling only to lean on secular principles as an alternative to sound doctrine. He wants families to be destroyed to rid the world of godly examples which reflect the relationship between God and His church. Satan delights in same-sex marriage because it hinders the course of natural reproduction and defies the laws of nature. Lucifer–Satan–thinks artificial intelligence is a perfect path for the world. What would be the need for love in a world of artificial intelligence where it could not be reciprocated? He wants mankind destroyed; so, why not start from within by destroying babies in the womb of mothers? Why wouldn't Satan want to destroy marriage with divorce? Isn't his goal to shake the foundations? These are serious points to ponder.

When approaching these daunting issues, Christian counselors should operate on the foundation of love while holding fast to the Word uncompromisingly. All too often, counselors make the dreadful mistake of judging while counseling. These judgments sometimes lead to condemning thoughts. Condemnation only lands the counselee in hell in the mind of the condemner. Counselors should be reminded that hopeless counseling is helpless. It is important to remain open to the limitless, working power of God through grace.

Dependency on God for Answering 21st Century Counseling Issues

We have already established that in the Christian counseling session, the counselor is always acting under the delegated authority of God. Hence, he or she acts like an ambassador for the kingdom of God. Therefore, his or her actions are subject to the King's instructions. These instructions are non-negotiable. The circumstances surrounding any counseling issue never determine if God's instructions are optional or his ability situational. Instead, God gives the specific direction for each situation. King David demonstrated the importance of listening to God, even when the situation seems very similar to the last. For the believer, wars of the flesh resurface from time to time. King David's battles with the Philistines were very similar. In 2 Samuel Chapter 5, the Philistines spread themselves in the Valley of Rephaim to attack David and his men.[240] Before going into battle, David inquired of the Lord. Note that this was not his first battle with the Philistines. In fact, he had been victorious in battle prior to this point. But before he would set out to do anything, David consulted with the Lord. The Lord reassured him that he would make him victorious, so David attacked the enemy and won. Not long after, the Philistines came again and spread in the Valley of Rephaim. Sometimes the enemies we go up against are seemingly relentless. The king could have simply used the same strategy that gained him victory in his prior defeat of his enemy. Wisely, he inquired of the Lord again. The second time, God gave him *different* instructions for how to defeat the same enemy in the same place! David's respectful regard for the Lord – not his own ability – resulted in victory. This same respectful regard should be practiced in counseling. The counselor should never lean on his or her own understanding. It is good to acknowledge the Lord for His wisdom in execution.[241]

Proper acknowledgment of God requires that His instructions are executed according to His way. This means that His decisions must be respected and accepted. Years ago, after fasting and praying for my father, who had been diagnosed with stage IV lung cancer, he died. As a registered respiratory therapist, I was well-trained in every aspect of the disease. Coupled with fasting and praying, I also did everything I could do according to medical knowledge to nurture him back to good health. Though the prognosis was poor, I endeavored to do everything to assist him with living. Fifteen months after being diagnosed, my father passed away, *anyway*. What did this mean for my faith? After all, I had fasted and prayed. Isn't that what a Christian is supposed to do in times of crisis? Not only did I fast and pray, but I used my medical skills at the bedside of my father. God still chose to receive him Tuesday, July 25, 2006. After receiving the news, I remember surrendering *my* expectations. After praying with my mother and settling at home, I decided to eat. I quickly recalled a passage of scripture where King David fasted for his sick son. King David's reaction at the news from his servants that his son had died, has always been startling for me. He got up from the floor, washed his face, combed his hair, changed clothes, went to worship in the sanctuary, and finally, he ate.[242] This is an act of surrender and acceptance. Accepting the will of God means that we will sometimes be left grieving our own expectations. In obedience to God, we must learn to accept the will of God even when it does not meet our personal wishes.

Often, when the will of God does not match or seemingly supersede our human expectation, human interference occurs. In the case of counseling, human interference occurs when the counselor or the counselee takes matters into his or her own hands. This leads to misapplication of the Word of God to justify one's desires or actions. Therefore, a word of caution is necessary for counselors to never promise what the outcome of counseling will be. Only the Sovereign God knows what the outcomes will be. The example of King David in the Valley of Rephaim supports this truth. God's will is not based upon human desires or past experiences. The poison of human interference can delay the process toward resolution of the counselee's issue(s).

Let's consider a few scenarios. Consider a Christian couple who has been praying to have a baby. There are many fertility options available for getting pregnant. Should the couple keep praying and wait even though they have already been waiting several years to conceive? Should the couple adjust their prayer to ask for the fertility drugs or procedures to work? Should the couple adopt and forget about conceiving altogether? The real question is, "What does the Word of God say about any of this?" Consider another couple who has conceived but has been told that termination of the pregnancy is necessary to save the mother's life. These are some of the questions that pastors, counselors, and those in need of guidance will be challenged with. Unfortunately, the answers to these situations have been based on the moral relative positions of the individuals in these situations. Both situations raise interesting arguments.

Several arguments can be made for the first couple (in no particular order):

- The couple should consider fertility options. Maybe God will work through the fertility doctor to recommend a solution. The doctor can be a vessel that God works through.
- Why pray for fertility options to work when they can simply pray that they conceive. Afterall, they are praying to the same God who can do anything and what is impossible with man is possible with God.

- They should adopt. Obviously, God wants them to do so because the Bible says true religion is to take care of the widow and the orphan, right?

Several arguments can be made for the second couple as well (in no particular order):

- The mother is already living, and her family knows and loves her. They really do not know the baby. So, terminate the pregnancy. Afterall, the baby is not born, right? Plus, the father would be left to raise the child and any other children alone.
- Do not terminate the pregnancy. God is the reason that conception even happened. God specializes in things which are impossible. Give it a chance. Keep praying for a miracle for both the mother and the baby.

When we consider these arguments, it can become very clear the dilemma that moral relativism causes in counseling. Many of the arguments, if presented alone, would sound plausible and reasonable. It is also possible to see the dilemma that Christians may face when having discussions regarding such matters. Many of the arguments seem to be supported by a scripture or biblical principle that may be familiar to the one experiencing the situation. This type of assumption may lead to making the wrong decision. It is not uncommon for Christians to use the Word of God to validate their personal wishes and desires. This is "scriptural malpractice." In such cases, Christian counselors should look for the most practical application of the Word of God. The search for absolutism is not always a clear path. The answer goes back to the act of asking God *first*. Even concerning what one may feel is the least or most minuscule thing, seeking God first is always the absolute right thing to do. The counselor is tasked with asking questions such as, "What did God say about this? Have you prayed about this?" When praying for an answer, it is important to remind the counselee to be open to the will of God. Referring to my father's death, I had to accept the will of God although I wanted nothing more than a miracle to occur. Counseling in the 21st century does not work if the counselor simply pulls the file of the last counselee who had the seemingly same or similar situation. Every case is a case for God. What He did in the last case, He may not choose to do in another one. Since my father's death, I have prayed for many people who were diagnosed with cancer and survived. I cannot explain why God allowed them to live and my father to die. I could easily speculate. However, my speculations are not absolute or universal. I do know that common to every case is the need to fully trust God for the answers. I also know that God's answers are non-negotiable.

We Cannot Neuter God

When answers are not clear cut and sitting on the surface so to speak, the need for digging deeper becomes more apparent. Still in digging deeper, the answers are not always obvious. One of the goals of practicing medicine is to identify the root cause of illnesses. Because the answer is often unknown, the doctor is left with treating the symptoms rather than the disease itself. Physicians are advised not to make diagnoses based on speculations alone. Often, further testing is necessary before rendering a final diagnosis. Meanwhile, the physician is careful to treat and monitor the related symptoms. If the physician fails to conduct further testing, he or she may commit malpractice. If a patient really needs a higher dose of medicine to treat an issue, but the physician has administered or prescribed a weaker dose, the patient risks not getting better or even getting worse although he or she is consuming medication. In counseling, it will be difficult to witness a breakthrough if the counselor does not apply the Word of God correctly. Therefore, the counselee does not get better by merely coming to counseling. He or she gets better by applying the *content* of counseling.

As mentioned in an earlier chapter, the Word is not a generic brand that can be used interchangeably or as a cheaper, less potent version of the truth. There is also no neutralizer for the Word. If it is to exist as it is, then it cannot be changed or altered. Any change or alteration means that it is no longer authentic. To neutralize means to render (something) ineffective or harmless by applying an opposite force or effect. In reference to the Word, to remove or add to it, will distort its original meaning. Since the it is settled in heaven, there is no need to revise it. The Word will stand without one jot or one tittle of it passing from the law until all be fulfilled.[243] Therefore, it cannot lose its power although attempts be made to alter it. However, those who make attempts to neutralize it, end up themselves being powerless. The uncompromised Word is the true source of power for believers.

When the Word is under attack, essentially God is under attack. As we have discussed, not every word in the Bible is spoken by God. However, the Bible contains the spoken words of God. Many will alter or misinterpret the Word to serve their own personal agendas. Many churches, or local assemblies, use "gender neutral" pronouns in place of the masculine he, him, and his. Some believe that the use of these pronouns to describe God sacralizes patriarchy.[244] On January 27, 2018, delegates at the Episcopal Diocese of Washington's 123rd Diocesan Convention passed a resolution to stop using masculine pronouns or "gendered language for God" in future updates to its Book of Common Prayer.[245] For some, the idea stems from the desire to be gender sensitive. Similar revisions are inclusive of referring to God as "Father." For centuries Christians have read passages where Jesus referred to God as "Abba." Such expressions continue to be of great debate.

The New International Version Bible, NIV, which according to the Christian Booksellers Association is a best-seller in English, has issued a new edition, the 2011 NIV. This edition replaced the 1984 edition. Several attempts have been made to revise the NIV. These attempts have met with much resistance from concerned

American evangelicals. The resistance is the result of the gender-neutral approach of the Today's New International Version, (TNIV) in 2002 and 2005. The 2011 NIV is a revision based on the TNIV-2005. Several of the gender-neutral translations were revised in the 2011 NIV. However only 25% were corrected and made gender-specific while 75% remained gender-neutral. Inaccurate translations totaled 3,686 when the TNIV Bible first appeared. According to Grudem and Thacker, only 933 were revised.[246] This leaves readers of the 2011 NIV yet susceptible to untruths. These so-called subtle changes to pronouns and proper nouns result in major translation errors.

In Martin Luther's 1524 treatise, "To the Councilmen of All Cities in Germany That They Establish and Maintain Christian Schools," he says,

> "And let us be sure of this: we will not long preserve the gospel without the languages [Hebrew, Aramaic & Greek]. The languages are the sheath in which this sword of the Spirit [Ephesians 6:17] is contained; they are the casket in which this jewel is enshrined; they are the vessel in which this wine is held; they are the larder in which this food is stored."[247]

Luther insisted on the importance of understanding and translating the Word based on the original text. Pastor Eric Anderson refers to translations which veer away the languages as being more like cheap toys rather than platinum.[248] Many translations such as the TNIV, NIV, Inclusion Version, and the New Revised Standard Version lean toward political correctness but are often not doctrinally sound making them theologically faulty.

There are several problems that are created when the Word is *revised* to become culturally inclusive, gender sensitive, or politically correct. When the Word is altered to meet the desires of the recipients, morals become *relative* but not necessarily *relevant*. The relevance of the text can easily be interpreted to mean something different from the original script. Again, moral relativism in many cases alters the moral relevance of scripture. The absolute value of scripture is as an unaltered original as inspired of the Holy Spirit to be written. Hence, the Holy Spirit's guidance is essential to the interpretive value of the Word. One of the areas of concern regarding pronoun alteration is in the reference of Jesus as "Son." Many argue that He should be referred to as the "child" of God. Others argue that God should have a neutral reference assigned to Him. These contenders often reference Genesis 17:1 as support for this claim. In this scripture, God reveals Himself to Abram as El Shaddai.[249] Some translate El Shaddai as Breasted One and use this as an argument for God being feminine, transgender, or neutral.[250] El Shaddai is translated more often to mean God Almighty. Those who are tempted to settle at the idea that God is the Breasted One without further examination, will be led to believe that God is identifying as female rather than referencing a robust chest as a symbol of strength. Readers should be cautioned to study the meaning of scripture and not just read it. To alter the gender references of God, will alter the meaning of the Bible. The Law required that the first-born son receive the inheritance of the Father. Another occasion that contesters use to validate their desires to be more inclusive of female pronouns and gender-sensitivity is when the daughters of Zelophehad fought to possess the land of their father.[251] There was no male next of kin in this case and each tribe was given the right to keep their land within their tribe. God gives Jesus as His only begotten Son.[252] The politically correct contenders suggest that Jesus should be referred to as "child" to be inclusive of both male and female who are saved and those who will accept Him. A strong counterargument should be made here. Christians forfeit the inheritance by neglecting to acknowledge the Word of God as it *is*. If it is manipulated to refer to Jesus as "child", then the Law *is not* fulfilled. Again, the Law required a first-born son. The Bible does not need to be altered to say "child." If altered, the promise cannot be fulfilled and the heirship according to Galatians 3:29 would be nullified. Jesus is Redeemer because He is the first-fruit from the grave and the only begotten *Son* of God. God orchestrates this with great purpose of fulfilling the Law so that the promise He made to Abraham would be fulfilled. Reference to Jesus as the Son of God in no way exempts a female from salvation. Consider how the prophet Isaiah acknowledges Jesus.[253] Isaiah says a "child is born" and "unto us a son is given." If every reference to Jesus is altered to say "child," Isaiah 9:6 would be redundant, and its meaning would be distorted. A "son is given" to those who will receive Him as Lord. Jesus is often referred to as the Son of Man and the Son of God. These two references are important when understanding that Jesus is Redeemer who satisfies the law and reconciles all God's children back to Him.

Altering holy scripture for preferential and political inclusion is problematic. The scripture does not need to be altered to be inclusive of women in ministry. The Bible is full of examples of women who work many aspects of the church. An understanding of the scripture as it is written, is more important than changing it. Deliberate changes to fit cultural preferences are unacceptable and rob the text of its true powerful meaning. If God is neutered and texts are altered, the mission of Jesus Christ and His work on Calvary will be nullified. For new converts, it is important that they began their Christian journey guided by a study through a plausible version of the Word. The absolutism of God is as such because He is who He is without the need for validation. Because He is absolute, His word is superior and the standard that this world needs.

The church, the Bride of Christ, places herself in great danger of suffering an identity crisis when she compromises on the Word. God's covenant with the church is a binding agreement that still stands because of His Son, Jesus. As with any contract, it is not to be altered. It is a legally binding document. Jesus is the only reason that the promises of God are still available to us. His redemptive power cannot be excluded. As our Counselor, Jesus represents believers before the righteous Judge, making us eligible heirs to the promise.

The identity crisis that is resulting from alteration of scripture is a trick of Satan to lead believers and those who *would* be saved to forfeit the promise.

Much emphasis is given to the change of pronouns and names here because these changes expose the church to so many untruths and practices which are contrary to the instructions in the Word. When the Body of Christ compromises on the seemingly basic things, it destroys the integrity of the church. Compromise and manipulation of the text is like tearing the skin of a human being. The skin is the largest organ system. While some people do not think it a big deal to receive a small cut on the skin, that small cut can become the entry point for many unwanted pathogens. These pathogens can lead to systemic sepsis of the *entire* body if not addressed in a timely manner. When sin is ruining the life of an individual, the medicine of God's Word is warranted. Just as it is necessary that the correct amount of medication be administered for the physical body, the same is true with Body of Christ. A diluted version of a God-ordained solution is useless. Pharmacists warn of the danger associated with cutting some pills. Taking a pill that has been cut in half in these instances can be dangerous to the patient. Compromise and "cutting" of the Word to fit one's personal desire is dangerous as well. Christian leaders, including Christian counselors, have a responsibility to hold fast the profession of faith without wavering and to ensure that the Word is properly applied like a healing salve.[254]

CHAPTER 8

LGBTQIAPK COMMUNITY

Issue of Love

Compromise of the gospel throughout the years has led to misinterpretation of the meaning of many biblical principles such as love and the institution of marriage. Consequently, there is an increase in the number of divorces among heterosexual couples, an increase in same-sex marriages, and an increase in hate crimes associated with sexual orientation. These all speak to the fact that people around the world do not love the same. It has been said that love is a universal language. This statement does not hold true today. Love means so many different things to so many different people. Whether based on culture, personal beliefs, or religious background, love is a subjective matter. Love's expression is like a kaleidoscopic mixture of these personal beliefs, cultural and societal behaviors, and religious and non-religious practices. On June 26, 2015 the United States experienced a historic shift of marriage to include same-sex marriage in America.[255] The nation now stands openly divided on the matter. With the growing number of hate crimes toward LGBT –lesbian, gay, bisexual, transgender – youth in America, much effort has been invested in anti-bullying campaigns, resource and assistance programs, depression therapy, and suicide prevention. The federal government and many other agencies have implemented many measures to support the rights of the LGBT community such as the first comprehensive National HIV/AIDS Strategy, legislative efforts to ban the use of "conversion therapy" against minors, an Executive Order by President Barack Obama prohibiting federal contractors from discriminating against any employee or applicant for employment because of race, color, religion, sex, sexual orientation, gender identity, or national origin, published Examples of Policies and Emerging Practices Guide for Supporting Transgender Students by the U. S. Departments of Education, and continual work at addressing LGBT housing discrimination.[256]

With the passing of time the abbreviation, LGBT, has lengthened and continues to grow with the increasing categories for sexual orientation and gender preference. For the sake of discussion here, the LGBTQIAPK COMMUNITY will be referenced. What does LGBTQIAPK mean? The abbreviation stands for lesbian, gay, bisexual, transgender, queer or questioning, intersex, asexual, pansexual, and kink. According to the American Addictions Center, the meaning of these is as follows:

- **LESBIAN** A female-identifying person who is sexually and romantically attracted to other female-identifying people.
- **GAY** Specifically, this word refers to a male-identifying person who is sexually and romantically attracted to other male-identifying people. Broadly, the word gay means any person attracted to people who have the same sexual identity.
- **BISEXUAL** A bisexual person is someone who is sexually and romantically attracted to both male and female-identifying people. People identifying as bisexual are not explicitly attracted to 50% male, 50% female people, but enjoy a spectrum of attraction.
- **TRANSGENDER** A transgender person is someone whose gender does not correspond with the sex with which they were born.

- **QUEER** The word queer is an inclusive term for someone who does not want to box in their sexual orientation or gender by labeling it.
- **INTERSEX** An intersex person is someone who was born a specific gender, but their biological sex (chromosomes, hormones, etc.) or reproductive organs are of the opposite sex.
- **ASEXUAL** Someone who identifies as asexual is a person who doesn't find a sexual attraction or interest in either sex. An asexual person might also have little interest in sexual activities as well, but this does not mean that they lack interest in or desire to foster intimate relationships with others.
- **PANSEXUAL** A person who identifies as pansexual is sexually and romantically attracted to people of all sexual and gender identities.
- **POLYAMOROUS** People who identify as polyamorous engage in open relationships with their sexual and romantic partners. These open relationships are mutual, respectful, and require consent from all parties involved.
- **KINK** Kink is an all-encompassing term to define those who enjoy participating in kinky sexual behavior. Kinky sexual behavior can involve anything from using a blindfold or tying each other up, all the way to far more painful activities. And while bondage, domination, and submission play a role in kink, there MUST ALWAYS be open lines of communication between consenting partners.[257]

Along with the expanding abbreviation for this community comes an expansion of drug and alcohol abuse, suicide, depression, broken families, unmet expectations, and much more. How will Christian counselors approach these challenges compassionately without compromise of the gospel? The church, as a whole, needs to be ready for this and many other issues which are becoming increasingly prevalent in the world today. Does the church simply separate from those who live in one of the categories within the LGBTQIAPK abbreviation? Is there a need for separation rather than confrontation?

A response in love *should* be the obvious start. One of the greatest desires and tricks of the enemy, Satan, is to pervert the meaning of love. Perversion is the parent of lust and other uncommon practices witnessed all too often in society. One can argue that perversion and its subtle connotations are so common in television and social media that people have either become accepting of it or numb regarding it. As a result, perversion is becoming an unaddressed norm. Christian counselors must be willing to address the fruit of perversion related to the LGBTQIAPK community, as well as the heterosexual community. Pornography, adultery, and fornication are seemingly passive behaviors widely accepted in society. Lust and self-love are the drivers for many sexual acts of sin which are committed. These distortions of true love are cautioned against in the Bible. The prophet Jeremiah warns that the heart is more deceitful than all else.[258] One who seeks to satisfy the urges of the flesh will ultimately engage in lustful deeds. These are selfish deeds that lead to fulfillment of fleshly desires. Nothing good dwells in the flesh.[259]

Christian counselors cannot avoid the address of these challenges. Like Jesus, counselors must address these maladies with love, the fundamental basis for Christian counseling and meeting needs. Therefore, it is beneficial for counselors to know the four types of love: Storge, Philia, Agape, and Eros. These various expressions of biblical love are intended to be the basis for human interaction. The scriptures are full of illustrative examples of these love types. Unfortunately, the world has managed to distort what these four forms of love mean. For example, *Storge* love, affectionate love, is the type of love that one has for someone he or she cares about.[260] This is the tender love a parent has for a child as evidenced in Isaiah 49:15.[261] With the continual debates surrounding abortion and women's rights around the globe, Storge love is not at the highest level of expression that it could be. When we consider the numbers of children sold, kidnapped, raped, abused, and or murdered, we can see that Storge love is not existing nearly at the level intended by God. The number of children in foster care and those who go homeless because they have been kicked out by parents who disown them due to their sexual orientation speaks to the dilemma surrounding Storge love. Christian counselors must prepare to work with parents who need assistance balancing love for their children while disagreeing with their choices.

Gun-violence in America is just one of the many indicators that mankind is experiencing a shift in kind regard for one another. Home invasions and armed robberies prove that some people love things more than they love their neighbor. Holy scripture urges that we consider others above ourselves.[262] This is not the case in a world drunk with the message of self-love and conceit. Those who subscribe to the idea of self-love with no regard for their fellow brother have a poor self-image often accompanied by poor self-esteem. The need for restoration of *Philia* love, love for one's brother, is critical in current times.[263] Cain is still killing Abel with no remorse for the blood on his hands or any regard for life.[264] Hate crimes are being committed where reconciliation nearly ceases to be. Racial tension has been fueled by the ongoing murders of African Americans in disturbing numbers at the hands of police officers. Police officers who seek to do good are being blamed and underappreciated due to the acts of a guilty few. Have we stopped to ponder the naked truth of a man or woman before he or she robes behind a badge and a uniform? Many in Muslim communities are treated poorly and harassed because of their religious and cultural backgrounds. Schools and workplaces are inundated with the constant conversation surrounding bullying and gun violence which claim the lives of our children by suicide and violent death. As many of their teachers die alongside them, we lose a generation of potential problem solvers along with our storytellers simultaneously. People going into abortion clinics have been killed and some harmed for their choice to kill an unborn baby. In those situations, who stops to think that the number of lives lost were two for one at the moment. Active shooters and drive-by shootings claim the lives of many innocent because of a hurting one. We cannot treat lives like some 2-for-1 special at a drive-thru window. When do angry protesters consider being loving proclaimers? The lack of brotherly love in the world leads to hurt. Hurt only hurts, having no regard for who it victimizes. The Christian counselor is tasked with addressing these issues. Caution must be taken on the behalf of counselors not to allow their personal beliefs to sway them toward one side of the issue leaving the other side unaddressed. Yet, counselors cannot swing on the pendulum of indecisiveness. They must apply the Word of God to each situation according to the leading of the Holy Spirit.

Biblical love types are overlapping in nature. Where Agape love does not abound, the potential for vengeful wrath does. Agape love is unconditional or persisting love for someone.[265] Although it is most often stated as unconditional, Agape love does not mean that one's sin is without consequence. Philia love would be more plentiful if people practiced more Agape love. Self-righteousness is often the hidden culprit working behind the scenes decreasing the amount of unconditional or persisting love. Self-righteous people tend to only have concern for themselves and their own outcomes. When conditions are not in their favor, pride erects a wall. People who have a difficult time letting go of or forgiving past hurt tend to lack in the practice of Agape love. Christian counselors must minister love in some of the most difficult cases. In prisons around the world, it is clear to see that just as much as people deserve to be locked up, they *need* to be loved. It is so easy to become so fixated on the infraction that God's purpose is left ignored or incomplete in the lives of people who we fail to help but who, yet we are so swift to judge. Often the focus is on the severity of the punishment rather than on the corrective nature of love. This is not to suggest that prison time served is wrong and that criminals should be made to feel better about their sin. However, it is an often-ignored truth that God is both the God of justice *and* love. Again, God is love.

The fourth love expression, Eros love or romantic love, is a "reserved" love.[266] By it being a reserved love, it is the love shared between two people in marriage. This type of love is a sexual love. God reserved sex for marriage. Sex, however, is often seen or implied to be permissible outside of marriage on television and on social media. Internet and dating services serve as the meeting place for people seeking sex without commitment to a relationship or marriage. Today, sex is so displaced from its original intent for marriage that it is like a fire outside of a fireplace. With the increasing number of people choosing to live together as couples without marrying, sex is even the more displaced from God's intended purpose. What we have as a result is *error* rather than Eros. Therefore, Eros love is easily substituted by lusts of the flesh. These lusts include, but are not limited to, swinging (where couples switch partners), adultery, and fornication. Some would argue that members of the LGBTQIAPK community have a distorted view of Eros love. By biblical standard, sexual relationships between two women or two men are considered unnatural passions.[267] However, these behaviors are becoming an accepted norm in mainstream society. Christian counselors are charged with the responsibility of addressing some of the toughest and most challenges topics of all time. Reverend Brian Scott, senior pastor of Union Baptist Church, Harlem, New York urges Christians to understand that we do not have a choice about what we are commanded to do, but we have a challenge! We cannot act as if we have a choice regarding obeying the Word of God. We *do* have to understand the challenges that need our proper address. Many of these topics are controversial because they are politically correct yet morally wrong. Unlike secular counselors, Christian counselors are not committed to being politically correct. However, true Christian counselors should counsel based on Jesus' example. Biblical counseling is an amazing opportunity for evangelism. Counselees can be won for Christ when love is at the center of uncompromised counseling. Love coupled with a pure motive that sees the counselee restored are biblical alternatives to methods which seemingly judge and criticize the counselee. Reproof and rebuke are vital to meeting these goals.[268] If the counselor follows the lead of the Holy Spirit, He [The Holy Spirit] will lovingly guide the process.

Counseling Considerations for the LGBTQIAPK Community

With a change in time comes a shift in the way people outside of the LBGTQIAPK community relate. In addition to "gender", acts of discrimination are now toward sexual orientation. Professed Christians who hold fast that God is absolute, seem to be a shrinking minority. Many Christians would rather resort to their self-made communities consisting of their private schools than to deal with the realities surrounding the openness of members of the LBGTQIAPK community. Let me assert that there is nothing wrong with private schools. I attended them and was fortunate to build a Christian foundation. However, there are several things for consideration. Christians who do not agree with the openness surrounding LGBTQIAPK preferences should ask themselves which would they prefer, a hidden/unknown "issue" or a known one? Neither covert nor overt behaviors of any sin lessen the fact that it is sin. God sees all things whether they be hidden from man or not. Sometimes Christians are so focused on sheltering themselves from sin, that the sin often goes without proper address, *even within themselves.* Condemnation without proper confrontation still leaves the issues unaddressed. Christians can hate sin and still lovingly confront it. Parents are challenged with raising children in a wholesome environment while having to deal with the risk of unwanted worldly messages invading the innocence of children through video games, television, and other sources. Christians are often viewed as being hateful and labeled as "non-inclusive" at the refusal to accept the "behaviors" associated with the LGBTQIAPK community. Some of these so-called "behaviors" are no different from what is witnessed among heterosexual identifying individuals. The issue is that Christians do not believe that these things should take place woman to woman or man to man. This is true. However, we must *also* address heterosexual sins or sin period. Not long ago, public display of affection was considered inappropriate by some societal rules or etiquettes. With the shift in time, public displays of affection are common to see. But who determines if it is acceptable or not? Apparently, there is still an ambiguity concerning acceptance and who makes the rules.

Be of good courage because there is a place for openness for all sinners and sufferers. That place is the Christian counseling setting. The dilemma is that many members of the LGBTQIAPK community, as also in the heterosexual community, do not believe they have a problem or that they have need for counseling at all. Some would probably contend that the need for counseling lies with Christians who "judge" them. The difficulty which goes along with counseling those who may not see a need for it is very evident. In situations where a loved one's desire for a family member or friend to receive counseling is unmet, the loved one can receive counseling to learn how to cope appropriately and respond in love to the nonconsenting family member. This does not suggest that agreement with the lifestyle is a point of settling. Counseling in these situations, would be a way of coaching as well. Children are sometimes kicked out and some run away from home when there is parental rejection of their sexual orientation. Parents who resort to kicking their children out of the home need counseling themselves. The purpose served in providing counseling for parents would be to arm them with the loving tools, support, and prayer necessary to work as agents of positive change.

Satan would love to see families destroyed and lives ruined. Hence, there is no room for conformity. Sexual orientation is clearly decided by the Creator. God, along, makes this determination. In Romans Chapter 12, the Apostle Paul admonishes believers to present their bodies a living sacrifice, holy, acceptable unto God.

Paul calls this "reasonable service."[269] This reasonable service, which is to be acted upon daily, is a part of the ongoing process of sanctification in the lives of believers. As Paul continues his address, he further warns believers not to conform to the world and to allow for transformative renewal of the mind.[270] Pausing here, it is clear that God does not intend for Christians to fall prey to the ways of the world. Conformity is not the answer. Contrary to the opinions and adopted beliefs of many, conformity and compromise are not acts of love. Confrontation is an act of love. In the latter part of Romans 12:2, Paul gives the reason that transformative renewal of the mind is important. Renewal of the mind is necessary for the believer to prove what is that good, and acceptable, and perfect, will of God.[271] Hence, the personal preferences of an individual are not the key focus or determinant of sexuality or gender. Instead, the focus of an individual should be nested in the will of God. Much of the focus in contemporary society is based on allowing everyone to have a seat at the table. Everyone is fighting for "their" right. There is nothing wrong with being just or fair regarding who has the seat at the table. However, the agenda on the table has shifted. No longer is God considered the chief executive officer, CEO, of how life should be lived. Remember it is God who prepares both the table and the agenda.[272] Instead, man is increasingly designing his own roadmap for how life should be lived. With so much focus on "who" has a chance at living a full life free of prejudices, biases, injustices, hate, etcetera, there has been less focus of *how* life should be lived to please God. As an African American woman, I am not here to give discount to any of these things because they are worth address. None of these will change for better where there is no moral compass and regard for others. Much of what is taught regarding self-esteem is that one loves himself or herself, but often at the cost of not obeying God. When we consider the entire matter of John Chapter 15, we will realize that "self" has to be intertwined in God in order to be fruitful and most of all healthy.[273] When "self," apart from God, is the focus, obeying God is not the bigger picture. If children are taught from an early age that pleasing God is superior to pleasing "self" and, also, better for "self" in the end, perhaps self-satisfaction would not be such a major focus. When one seeks to satisfy self, lust wins.

God often gets blamed for uncontrolled lusts of the flesh. Because plausible explanations are not easily given for the reason(s) someone may be a member of the LGBTQIAPK community, it is often deemed as God's fault. Some people would just rather settle at they were born that way and leave it as such. Everyone is born in sin and shaped in iniquity, but none are expected to remain in the state of sin.[274] However, many supporters and members of the LGBTQIAPK community contend that their sexual orientation is not sin at all. Such conclusion allows for the freedom to be who they desire to be as opposed to who God designed them to be. The flesh's desire often distorts our view and distracts us from being obedient to the will of God for our lives. Tim Stafford says,

> "The flesh–that is, our lives without God–urgently desires may things. It wants power. It wants pleasure. It wants wealth. It wants status and admiration. None of these is wrong in itself. And nothing would be wrong with liking these things. But desire or lust is more than liking. It is the will to possess. Lust turns good things into objects of worship. And that is why lust or covetousness, is so closely linked to another biblical word: idolatry. What we lust for we worship. We may joke about our lust, but our behavior shows a more fundamental allegiance. We look to our idols to give us what we need–to make our lives rich and purposeful. In our culture an idol many people look to is the god of sexual fulfillment."[275]

From Stafford's comment we can gather that an individual is slave to his or her own personal desires when the flesh is allowed to lead and guide the course of life. The desire of the flesh is lust. To validate these actions, some people superimpose the meaning of love upon their lustful desires.

Christian counselors are charged with the task of guiding counselees who are members of the LGBTQIAPK community toward replacing one desire, flesh, with another one, holiness. Before going any further in this discussion, it is important to note that lusts are not exclusive to sexual sin. Just as Paul encouraged the Colossians to put away sexual immorality, impurity, lust, evil desires, and greed, which is idolatry, so must the counselor encourage the counselee to put away these things which belong to the earthly nature.[276] The ultimate desire of believers should be to please God. Consequently, salvation is important for effective counseling. If the desire of an individual is not to please God, he or she may easily be given over to the lusts of the flesh. The flesh always seeks to satisfy "self." Hence, the ongoing work of salvation through sanctification is paramount to victorious living.

Same-sex Marriage: Is this really marriage?

New developments over the last decade have caused, if not forced, the church and many businesses to consider new inclusions and clients. With the passing of new laws to allow for same-sex marriage in the United States, businesses and churches find themselves with the possibility of being accused of discrimination for refusal to serve those who desire to be married to someone of the same sex. To protect their religious beliefs, many churches have amended their constitution and bylaws secondary to the changes in legislation. These amendments have not all been in the same direction regarding the topic. Inclusion for some churches means including in the constitution and bylaws strong statements that state that according to their religious and/or scriptural beliefs, same-sex marriages will not be performed by the clergy or any other affiliate of that church.

Some churches are welcoming of same-sex marriages openly now with the changes in law. With the wake of same-sex marriage and the Supreme Court's decision in Obergefell v. Hodges, in which the court held that states must issue licenses for same-sex marriages and recognize such licenses issued by other states, many pastors became concerned about the possibility of being forced to solemnize, host, or perform same-sex ceremonies.[277] To date, pastors are protected under the First Amendment. The attack on religious freedom in America is highly anticipated. To avoid conflict and in many cases proper address of same-sex marriage, many churches have adapted to the addition of words such as inclusive and variations of the terms unity (unitarian) and universal (universalist) in the titles or names of church assemblies. The use of these terms in some cases is to identify as assemblies which accept members of the LGBTQIAPK community.

There is a misconception regarding the acceptance of members of the LGBTQIAPK community in churches. Many churches who are said not to accept members of the LGBTQIAPK community argue that they are not discriminative to any person. However, these churches are clear that the lifestyle and beliefs surrounding same-sex marriage and other practices associated with the lifestyle will be challenged scripturally as sin. In such case, the individual may be welcomed by the church assembly with the understanding that the lifestyle will be considered as sin as are other sins that perhaps other members or churchgoers have present in their lives. Assemblies which are said to be "accepting" may refer to the behaviors, beliefs, and lifestyles of members of the LGBTQIAPK as being okay. These assemblies are more likely not to address these behaviors, beliefs, and lifestyles as sin at all. There are some assemblies who may not allow for members of the LGBTQIAPK community.

Debates are ongoing regarding the church and same-sex marriage inclusion. These debates will continue because there is no consensus regarding where the church stands regarding the challenging issues of contemporary times. Some denominations have chosen to allow for its leadership to be accepted as members of the LGBTQIAPK community. Other denominations stand on the premise that being a member of the LGBTQIAPK community is abominable. With the varying stances by the church on this and other issues, confidence in organized religion is dwindling. The church's true identity is currently up for debate. Will the real church please stand up? How does the church recover? The answer is absolute. It is in the Word of God which is the absolute authority on Christian living, church operation, and determination of how to handle and address sin and other situations. While the church and the world are trying to figure things out, the Word is already written out. *For it is written.* Whether it is to accommodate for one's own desire or ignorance, it is never permissible to compromise the commands and instructions of God. Again, the work of the Holy Spirit is vital to counseling and decision making. The debate over same-sex marriage and other challenging issues in society should be no problem for the church who serves Jesus Christ. To apply a portion of the Bible without regard for the other, is sin itself. Compromise in this manner is sin. No one reserves the right to edit what God, Editor in Chief of our lives, has written and planned for mankind. God's Word is non-negotiable.

Marriage is an institution of God. It is not an institution created or coined by mankind. The creation of Adam and Eve is the intentional work of God and no mistake. God purposefully made woman from the rib he had taken out of the man.[278] God very well could have created without extracting man's rib to do so. He simply could have made her in the same manner that He created man. God intentionally made woman with this rib purposely having in mind the covenant that Christ and the church, His bride, would share. Several conclusions can be drawn here. Bone is the physical part of human beings which consists of living cells. Some bone houses bone marrow which is a spongy tissue containing stem cells. These stem cells can form into red blood cells, white blood cells, and platelets. Cells are the basic building blocks of all living things. God took the most important part of a man to make a woman. Analysis of bone tissue reveals that the very things necessary for optimal health and life are contained therein. Adam recognized Eve as bone of his bone and flesh of his flesh.[279] The better covenant is in the new testament of Jesus' blood.[280] Jesus, the Second Adam, connects believers to a better covenant through His blood shed and sacrifice at Calvary. Again, the Godhead –the Father, the Son, the Holy Ghost – cannot be neutered. Jesus, the Son of God, is the only one who can atone for the sins of human beings. The law required a male. The principle is seen clearly in the Book of Ruth. Ruth's husband, the son of Naomi, was dead. Naomi's husband and sons were dead at the onset of the Chapter 1. A kinsman redeemer was necessary for the women to live on and be provided for. God could have allowed Naomi and Ruth to marry if same-sex marriage was permissible in His sight. However, He did not allow for such. He was intentional about how the ancestors of Jesus would thrive. Boaz was the kinsman redeemer and without him, Ruth and Naomi were destitute. Jesus, also referred to as the Son of David because of His ancestry leading from Ruth, is the Redeemer.[281] Efforts to neuter the Godhead are efforts to neutralize the gospel. A neutral gospel would be indifferent and indecisive. Any attempts by the church to comply with or adapt to new cultural norms would lead to great compromise. The Word is all encompassing and interminable for all times. While it may not be the preferred answer in contemporary culture, it is definitely the necessary answer.

Any attempt to neutralize or water down the Word is an attempt to extract its power. Power is necessary to produce. The church cannot be an effective organism apart from the power of the Holy Spirit. Let us survey the gospel of John Chapter 15. Jesus, The Second Adam, does not speak of a covenant on physical terms as in Genesis 2:23. He reconciles mankind back to God and uses the analogy of the vine instead of bone and flesh to demonstrate how man connects with God.[282] The church, the bride of Christ, cannot have the power to produce *apart* from God. As Tim Stafford stated, flesh, simply stated, is life without God. Therefore, the first Adam could not atone for the sins of mankind meaning that mere man would not be able to save. God, Himself, would have to pay the ransom for atonement. The world needed a redeemer. The world needed a male heir to the throne of King David. Because Jesus is the Son of God and the Son of David, the heirship of the believer is irrefutable. In John Chapter 15, Jesus is identified as the true vine and God, the Father, as the vinedresser. Jesus refers to those who will come to believe in Him as branches and urges the branches to remain in Him to bear fruit. He is repetitive in urging the believer to abide in Him and allow Him to abide within the believer.[283] Jesus is intentional about the identification of the believer as a branch and Himself as the vine. His intentionality is as such to stress the functions of both the believer and his Lord in the covenant relationship. Jesus even states that the branch cannot bear fruit on its own. This concept is very important. Counseling that compromises on entire use or subjective use of the scripture is obsolete and will not produce fruitful results. Counseling of this sort is powerless; and therefore, fruitless. When the church, the bride of Christ, compromises, she becomes fruitless. However, God is faithful and loyal regarding His covenant.

What does same-sex marriage have to do with the covenant between Christ and the church? Well, marriage is the institution of God that is both legally and spiritually binding. Marriage between man and woman mirrors Christ and the church. When man and woman are married, the power to produce is possible. Satan would love for mankind made in the image and likeness of God to cease to exist. Same-sex marriage denies the possibility for natural reproduction. Consequently, same-sex marriage serves the desires of Satan and not the plan of God. The fact that two people of the same sex are not created physically for the act of sex speaks to the fact that Creator did not intend for them to interact sexually.

If we look at God's intention by studying His will for mankind, same-sex marriage is not marriage at all. Many would argue differently and to the contrary. The union of two people of the same sex does not agree with God's purpose in creation. When God commanded Noah regarding the animals that he should take with him on the ark, He told him to take by sevens a male and female of all the clean animals. This meant that Noah was going to take seven *pairs*. The female was counted as one with the male. The total would be fourteen, but God referred to the female as one with her male counterpart. Of the unclean animals, he commanded him to take by two of the animals, a male and its female. This is the way that the offspring of the earth would be preserved. God is purposeful and intentional. In Genesis 1:27, it says that God created man in his own image and in the image of God "created he *him*".[284] (emphasis mine) The verse goes on to reveal that he created *them* male and female. The New International Version Bible confuses this to say that God created mankind in his own image, in the image of God he created *them* rather than *him*. Verse 28 goes on to say that God blessed them and said be fruitful, multiply, replenish the earth, subdue it, and have dominion over the fish of the sea, over the fowl of the air, and over every living thing that moves upon the earth.[285] It seems that God is speaking blessings to the generations that will come from male and female. Eve is not created until chapter two of Genesis. Why would God bless "them" in verse 28 of Chapter 1 if Adam is not put to sleep until Chapter 2? The first Adam had in him the generations to come. He bore the seed. God intended for them to be fruitful. In John 15, the Second Adam admonishes believers to abide in Him.[286] In Him we have all we need to produce. For the believers to produce the greater works, we have to abide in Jesus and allow Him to be at home within our hearts.

According to Genesis 2:24 and Matthew 19:5, same-sex unions are not marriages. These verses are clear that God created male and female for one another. In Chapter 19 of the Gospel of Matthew, Jesus is questioned by Pharisees who had hoped to trap Him with a question about divorce.[287] Jesus had already addressed this matter in Chapter 5. The plot of the Pharisees was to disprove Him. They wanted to lead Jesus to go against the law of Moses. Jesus had already stated in Chapter 5 that he did not come to destroy or abolish the law of Moses or the prophets, but to fulfill it. Jesus was explicitly clear that until heaven and earth pass not one jot, or one tittle will pass from the law until all is fulfilled. Christian leaders and counselors should follow the example of Christ when it comes to addressing such challenging topics. Had Jesus compromised, the Pharisees would have taken occasion to judge as they so desired. They would have attempted to define right and wrong according to their self-righteous standard. God, Creator of heaven and earth, is the only person who determines what marriage is. He created the physical characteristics of male and female for natural connection with another. Individuals born of the same sex do not have physical reproductive characteristics which allow for natural or physical connection. Consequently, same-sex marriage is ungodly because these couples cannot fulfill the command of God which is to be fruitful and multiply. As in Noah's day, the earth cannot be replenished by same-sex couples. This unnatural union hinders reproduction.

Those who subscribe to the idea of same-sex marriage may very well argue that these couples can parent. However, parenting will not be the result of natural sexual means as God so intended for marriage between a woman and a man. Of course, science has evolved to allow mankind to do some pretty amazing things. Among these relatively new scientific developments is the ability to help parents with alternative means for conceiving. Besides becoming a parent because of a former relationship (usually past heterosexual), current relationship with someone who has a child, or adoption, members of the LGBTQIAPK community also consider donor insemination, reciprocal in vitro fertilization, and surrogacy. The problem with these methods is that they are a manipulation of the natural process instituted by God. Manipulation of the natural process for reproduction is not the equivalent of a reversible process such as changing one's hair color. Prevalent among many of these couples is one person who has tendency more toward behaving like the opposite sex. Consequently, psychological self-manipulation is very common. Inevitably, these individuals are at risk of losing themselves while trying to satisfy self, ego, or desires.

The Identity Crisis

Earlier, the "pronoun" dilemma was mentioned. As a review, many members of the LGBTQIAPK community prefer to be referred to by varying pronouns. Some individuals who were created female would prefer the pronouns "he, him, and himself" as opposed to "she, her, and herself." The reverse holds true for individuals created male. There are even individuals who desire to be referred to as "they, them, and themselves." In such case, the individual may have decided not to lean predominantly toward either gender. Many human resource departments are hosting diversity-inclusion trainings to teach employees gender sensitivity when communicating with customers and fellow employees. Many companies host these trainings in hopes of preventing lawsuits due to alleged discrimination.

Is it possible for held-on to concessions to result in some major issues? How psychologically healthy is this for children in schools? Can these preferences of pronoun identifications result in harm for one's physical health? There are so many issues to explore and questions to answer regarding the chosen identity of members of the LGBTQIAPK community. Christian leaders and counselors may not be given a seat at the table to discuss these issues, but they certainly must take a stand for the sake of humanity. Much of the identity crisis which is widespread in contemporary times has made its way into the church. Even schools have been on the slippery slope downward since the nineteenth century. Steven K. Green, constitutional historian and law professor, notes in his book *The Bible, the School, and the Constitution* that the decision made by the United States Supreme Court on June 25, 1962 in *Engel v. Vitale* that a prayer approved by the New York Board of Regents for use in schools violated the First Amendment by constituting an establishment of religion was not the beginning of the downward slope.[288] Waggoner referenced the histories of the Cincinnati "Bible Wars" of 1869-73 in his narrative to demonstrate that the debate of religion in schools has been ongoing. As the debate over religion in schools seems to be muffled by other cries of inequity, discrimination, sexism, misogyny, and racism, school shootings and other tragic events are increasingly prevalent in the United States.

Erik Erikson, German American developmental psychologist and psychoanalyst, is accredited with coining the term "identity crisis." His theory of personality houses eight life-stage virtues which describe stages of personality development by maturation.[289] Stage five – Fidelity, Identity vs. Role Confusion – looks at an individual during adolescent years, characterized by ages twelve through eighteen years old.[290] Erikson says that this is the stage of questioning whereby the adolescent asks "Who am I" and other similar things. The child seemingly pays more attention to himself or herself by surveying personal beliefs, goals, and values. He or she begins exploring morality through his or her own lens. Erikson believed that parents should allow for these explorations which he believed allows the child to determine his or her *own* identity. On the contrary, he believed when parents coerce the child to fulfill the parents' desires, the child is subject to an identity confusion. According to Erikson, this could result in a fidelity issue because the child would not learn to accept others even when they are different.[291] After all, the parent who pushes the child to be what the parent wants him or her to be is not teaching the child to accept people the way that they are. Erikson believed that an identity crisis arises from role confusion in cases where the child is not able to try out different lifestyles.[292] What if prayer and teaching religion in schools were priorities for children matriculating through stages one through four, characterized by children less than twelve years old? Perhaps a proper foundation would be laid for the child to make godly decisions and wiser ones. Some of the questioning that is believed to happen during the adolescent stage would not take place if the children had been taught his or her identity based upon the foundation of God's Holy Word. A lot of rebellion can possibly be prevented at this stage if there is already a knowledge of who Jesus is.

Attempts to secularize the Bible cannot be ignored. The church must endeavor to keep the Word of God untainted by the revisions which only seek to serve man's personal agenda. Members of the LGBTQIAPK community have an identity crisis as it relates to who God created them to be. The need to justify one's personal desires results in a few things such as recreating one's self and even revising the Bible. The latter is an attempt to alter biblical meaning to fit one's lifestyle. In fact, the very opposite is what should happen. One's lifestyle should be altered to align with the Word of God. Members of the LGBTQIAPK community are not the only individuals suffering from an identity crisis. Many heterosexual individuals subscribe to the ideology of being able to "recreate" one's self. Contemporary culture focuses of self rather than others. The need to recreate one's self is often the result of a constantly changing focus. Focus often changes based upon societal trends. God is the only constant in life. Being rooted and grounded in Him helps to stabilize those who experience shifts in their identity. Paul urges us in Philippians 3:14 to keep our eyes focused on the prize. What has God shown you? When we are off centered from His commands, we live apart from His promises.

The church of God is suffering from an identity crisis. Where there is compromise there is no standard. When the church compromises on the Word of God, there is no true foundation. First Samuel Chapter 4 is a prime example of what happens when the flesh is undisciplined and allowed to rule. In chapter 2 of 1 Samuel, Eli's sons were reported to lay with the women that assembled at the door of the tabernacle of the congregation.[293] After Eli admonished them, they continued to sin. In Chapter 4, Israel went out against the Philistines (flesh) in battle. Hophni and Phinehas, were found with the Ark of the Covenant which is the holy thing.[294] The Philistines were able to gain victory over Israel because their leaders thought they could handle the holy thing of God and yet continue in sin. The sons of Eli compromised. This cost them the battle against the Philistines. So, it is with flesh. When the church compromises, we lose the battle against the flesh and evil. Further in the text, Phinehas's wife has a baby while dying and she names him Ichabod, meaning the glory has departed[295]. The church can learn from this. It is not enough to do and produce. As those in covenant with God, we should seek to reproduce the things of God that bring glory to Him. The sin of homosexuality does not produce the things of God. Now let me be clear. Homosexuality is not the *only* sin in the church. It is just *one* of the topics in this work. Phinehas and his wife indulged in a heterosexual relationship and still produced Ichabod. Having a form of godliness is not enough. Going through the motions is not enough.

Phinehas's wife was dying while giving birth to her son. This is the picture of the church secularized and separated from God. The Apostle Paul in Romans 1:27 talks about men who receive in themselves the recompense of their error which was met.[296] It is clear that these men risked disease. When the Body of Christ compromises her identity, the entire body is at risk. Again, when the integrity of our physical skin has been broken or compromised, the entire body is at risk for infection and ultimately sepsis if not handled.

The attempt to neuter God by changing pronouns and by gender-sensitive revisions is evil. These attempts cause harm especially to individuals who are struggling with identity. God clearly speaks everything into existence. He formed Adam, and from Adam, he created Eve. He spoke over them in Genesis Chapters 1 and 2. The Father has already predetermined who we are. Our identity cannot be based on culture and other biases or experiences. Our culture has to be based on who we are – kingdom. We must be convinced that we are who God says we are. Ephesians 2:1–10 is a great biblical account of who believers are in Christ Jesus. Christian counselors must be mindful to share this passage and similar ones which share who we are because of Jesus. Being justified by faith in Christ Jesus is our identification with Him.[297] The belief that self-centered individuals must recreate themselves should be met with the need for sanctification instead. Sanctification is the ongoing remodeling which leads the believer to living better each day. Identify confusion is the result of idealistic distortion and the mistake of viewing life through rose-tinted lenses. When the reality of God's will and Word are embraced, the need for Jesus becomes more relevant. With the acceptance of the need for Christ, an individual will be better able to embrace a new identity in Him. First Corinthians 6:15 (KJV) says, "Know ye not that your bodies are the members of Christ? shall I then take the members of Christ, and make them the members of an harlot? God forbid." He admonishes believers to flee fornication and acknowledge the body as the temple of the Holy Spirit. Paul further tells them, "What? know ye not that your body is the temple of the Holy Ghost, which is in you, which ye have of God, and ye are not your own?"[298] Paul closes by reminding believers of the sacrifice of Jesus Christ in paying the price for salvation. This proves that no one has the right to change or alter his body or his being. We are who and what God says.

Christian counselors should always beware of the often undercover, narcissistic plot to hinder the will of God. Flesh must die daily. John 4:24 (KJV) says, "God is a Spirit: and they that worship him must worship him in spirit and in truth." When flesh is fed more than the spirit, the flesh will rule. The resulting issue is that the individual may feel the need to appease the flesh. This leads to idolatry and pride. Gay pride events *and* other similar events are examples of how the flesh further enhances the need to be validated. That need to be validated leads to narcissistic behaviors. Mistakenly, yet with good intentions, we think it is good to tell a child that he or she can be whatever he or she desires to become. This misguided statement leads children to fall into the trap of believing that identity is based on affiliations, careers, membership in social groups, and other similar things. Ultimately, we should pray for children asking

God early on to guide the course of destiny. Generally, we are guided by the power to be what we want to be. In the plight to be the perfect "self," we become the worst version of ourselves. If a person can embrace his or her flawed self and see the need for Jesus, that person is much better off.

Contemporary times are inundated with the need to wear labels. Culturally, the more labels a person takes, the seemingly more diverse and notable that person is. However, these labels do not add value to the individual. Contrarily, these labels reduce the individual to the definition (sometimes ever-changing definition) of the label itself. This leads to further identity distortion. Christians should not desire labels which are not compatible with their professed identity in Christ.[299] So many people seek self-worth and uniqueness by being labeled by a plethora of titles from the type of diet they consume to their highest level of academic achievement. These labels are often subdivided into more unnecessarily complex divisions. The church is not exempt of these labels which separate. Denominational divisions are multiplying as members of each group allow doctrinal beliefs to further separate them. The term denomination is a derivative of the term denominator, which is a mathematical term used to describe fractions. When believers are content to take a fraction of the Word of God for personal benefit and leave the rest, the Body of Christ is left fragmented and without unity. The Apostle Paul speaks to this in Ephesians 4:3–6 (KJV), "Endeavouring to keep the unity of the Spirit in the bond of peace. There is one body, and one Spirit, even as ye are called in one hope of your calling; one Lord, one faith, one baptism, one God and Father of all, who is above all, and through all, and in you all." God has called the church to wholeness and oneness in Christ Jesus. Sin and deception leave mankind depleted, broken, and out of relationship with God. The entire second chapter of the book of Ephesians shares the identity of the Christian through Christ Jesus. The identity of believers is expressed in 1 Peter 2:9 (KJV), "But ye are a chosen generation, a royal priesthood, an holy nation, a peculiar people; that ye should shew forth the praises of him who hath called you out of darkness into his marvellous light;"

Because we are chosen, we should not choose anything aside from God's will. While man has the free will of choice, it will cost him his salvation if he does not choose Christ. We have been called by God to be a royal priesthood. Hence, the church must endeavor to preserve the peace we have because of Jesus Christ. He is our peace.[300] To break covenant with Him by attempting to change the Word of God by means of neutering God and adding pronouns for gender-sensitive purposes, we negate our peace with Him and invoke the His wrath. Could some of these very acts of disobeying God be the reason that at the time of this writing we are experiencing global pandemics COVID-19 and racism? In 2020, we still have gender inequality, age discrimination, and the list *grows* on. First Peter 2:9 refers to believers as a holy nation. That reference is because of the believer's identity through Christ. It is important to clarify 1 Samuel 2:2 where it says that "there is none holy as the Lord: for there is none beside thee: neither is there any rock like our God."[301] Clearly, this means that the requirement of holiness can only be fulfilled by being in Christ Jesus. Apart from Him there is no holiness. Satan's attempts to alter the Word are means for separating men from the saving power and presence of God. This is the same trick that Satan used in the Garden of Eden. Because of Adam and Eve's failure to obey God, we were fallen. Without Jesus' redemptive work at Calvary, we would still be trapped in darkness. Modern day contemporaries who subscribe to the idea of enlightenment would contend that their knowledge and intellect have led them to the light. However, anything that leads an individual away from Jesus only leads that individual to darkness. You do know that you can be woke and yet exist in darkness? Many people are living out a night season believing that it is day. Jesus declares that He is the Light of the world and that those who follow Him will not walk in darkness but will have the light of life.[302] Anyone who denies the

Word of God, denies Jesus. This truth is supported by John 1:1-5 (KJV) which says,

> "In the beginning was the Word, and the Word was with God, and the Word was God. The same was in the beginning with God. All things were made by him; and without him was not any thing made that was made. In him was life; and the life was the light of men. And the light shineth in darkness; and the darkness comprehended it not."

When this passage of scripture is explored with integrity, it reveals that life is in God alone. It is also evident that the life is the light of men. John 10:10 reveals that Jesus came that men would have life and have it more abundantly.[303] Jesus is God; therefore, He is being referenced in John 1:1–3.[304] John 1:14 (KJV) supports this truth because it says, that "And the Word was made flesh, and dwelt among us, (and we beheld his glory, the glory as of the only begotten of the Father,) full of grace and truth." Verse fourteen indisputably reveals that Jesus, who is God, is the Word made flesh. When Jesus abides in the believer and the believer abides in Him, the Word dwells within the believer.[305] How can it be permissible to revise the Word to fit man's unrighteous desires? Jesus (the Word made flesh) cannot be altered by man. God cannot be changed by man. He is Creator and cannot be created. He is not likened unto a golden calf or some carved idol.[306]

Those who are created should not worship that which they create. God is the only Creator of mankind as noted in the first three chapters of the Book of Genesis. Idolatry stems from heart of man to control and or compete with God. When man realizes that God is incomparable and cannot be controlled, he seeks to alter God or create his own god. God is so absolute and sovereign that He swears only by Himself and not of anyone else.[307] His Word has been tried in the fiery furnace of all time and yet holds true. Calvinist theologian Theodore Beza (1519–1605) stated resolutely to the King of Navarre, "It belongs to the church of God to receive blows rather than to inflict them–but, she is an anvil that has worn out many hammers."[308] Beza, one of the most important leaders of the French Protestants in the 16th century, spread the gospel amidst strong resistance. With the turn of every century and with the implementation of every piece of legislation, the Word of God remains consistently true and withstands every attack. Therefore, believers must remain diligent to its preservation. Believers have a responsibility to hold fast to the truths of the Word by denouncing idols. Those who suffer from identity distortion cannot be allowed to control the interpretation of holy scripture. Throughout history, the fight to disprove the Bible has persisted but it has not prevailed. The impending wrath of God always causes the enemy to fear. Those who refuse to submit to God will seek to galvanize all who will fall prey to their false unity and empty encouragement. Isaiah 41:6-7 (KJV) illustrates this plainly, "They helped every one his neighbour; and every one said to his brother, Be of good courage. So the carpenter encouraged the goldsmith, and he that smootheth with the hammer him that smote the anvil, saying, It is ready for the sodering: and he fastened it with nails, that it should not be moved." As mentioned already, it is a Christian responsibility to endeavor to keep the unity of the Spirit in the bond of peace. When believers act indifferently, those who fight against the truth of God's Word continue with a united front. With this united front, they can influence changes to policies, practices, and law. Historically, those who have challenged the Word of God have stood encouraging one another. When individuals seek to protect their own desires, they find those who possess the common desire to stand with them. The LGBTQIAPK community has done so in the fight for legislation to approve same -sex marriage and other protections. Scripture records that those who build their idols would often solder and nail them so they would not fall out of place or be moved. The handiwork of man necessary to hold his god in place is evidence that no idol can compare to God the Father. It also says that these idols cannot stand on their own. Believers can be confident that the kingdom of God is unshakable and immovable.[309]

Christians should not passively say that the kingdom of God will always stand without actively working to ensure that it does. There is a responsibility to steward well the gifts of God which He freely gives to those who place their trust in Him. Hence, Christians must stand firm in the faith without compromise. Nothing will ever be comparable to the power, prominence, and presence of God. The men of Ashdod would attest to this fact. The Philistines took the ark of God and brought it from Ebenezer unto Ashdod. They placed the holy ark in the house of Dagon, their god, and set it beside Dagon. What happens as a result proves the inferiority of all gods to God. First Samuel 5:3–5 (KJV) records,

> "And when they of Ashdod arose early on the morrow, behold, Dagon was fallen upon his face to the earth before the ark of the Lord. And they took Dagon, and set him in his place again. And when they arose early on the morrow morning, behold, Dagon was fallen upon his face to the ground before the ark of the Lord; and the head of Dagon and both the palms of his hands were cut off upon the threshold; only the stump of Dagon was left to him. Therefore, neither the priests of Dagon, nor any that come into Dagon's house, tread on the threshold of Dagon in Ashdod unto this day."

Anything that is not of God cannot stand in His presence. All will fall in His presence. Every knee will bow, and every tongue will confess that Jesus is Lord.[310] The men of Ashdod quickly recognized that the hand of God was heavy against them. They realized that the ark could not remain among them if they were going to continue to worship Dagon.

Christian leaders and counselors are responsible to rely upon God and act at His will. The role of the counselor is designed to lead the counselee in identifying himself or herself through Jesus Christ. Our Savior was despised and rejected.[311] However, He actively completed His assignment at Calvary. We, who are made in His image, must endeavor in the work of grace.

CHAPTER 9

ABORTION

Same-sex marriage, suicide, sterility, the use of contraceptives, warfare, and abortion are just a few of the destructive venues of Satan to kill, steal, and destroy. Abortion, the deliberate termination of a human pregnancy, most often performed during the first 28 weeks of pregnancy, is a topic of legal debate.[312] While the legal arguments surrounding the topic get tossed back and forth by legislators, the church seems to be a little less aggressive about the matter. Many have argued that abortion is not a legal issue but instead, a moral one. The issue has caused great unrest coupled with protests. Women's right activists contend that a woman's body is not legal property and that women should be able to make a decision of their choice. These activists and other pro-choice individuals believe that women have the basic human right to decide when and whether to have children, based on their own moral and religious beliefs, even though they (pro-choice supporters) themselves may not choose abortion as an option for an unplanned pregnancy.[313] Pro-life activists oppose abortion and euthanasia. Planned Parenthood claimed that 1 in 4 women in the United States will have had an abortion by age 45.[314] However, Guttmacher Institute discovered that the abortion rate for women ages 15 to 44 dropped by 13 percent between 2008 and 2011.[315]

According to the Planned Parenthood webpage in 2019-20, abortion is stated as a very safe procedure.[316] Surely, Planned

Parenthood has not taken into consideration both the psychological and physical complications suffered by women post-abortion. According to the World Health Organization, WHO, nearly 70,000 women die each year as result of the complications from illegal or unsafe abortions.[317] This data does not consider the number of complications and deaths suffered by women who undergo "legal" abortions. According to abortion surveillance findings and reports, 623,471 legal induced abortions were reported to the Centers for Disease Control and Prevention (CDC) from 48 reporting areas in 2016.[318] While abortions are still legal in many parts of the United States, the number of abortions has hit the lowest since the Roe v. Wade Supreme Court ruling.[319] The decline that was reported was seen across all age groups of women.

The number of deaths of both women and children due to abortion along with complications of the procedure seem to be ignored by abortion activists. So many questions revolve around the subject. Planned Parenthood considers itself a trusted health care provider, and informed educator, a passionate advocate, and a global partner helping similar organizations around the world. How can Planned Parenthood consider itself as a care giver when the death of innocent, unborn babies is its specialty? How can Planned Parenthood consider itself as a passionate advocate? To those who disagree with the pro-choice agenda, there is no passionate advocacy on the behalf of an organization who kills children and risks destroying the womb and the spirit of the mother. Furthermore, Planned Parenthood's name is misleading. Services rendered by the organization do not support parenthood at all. How can you be a parent without the child who makes you one? Real planned parenthood is according to God, the Creator of mankind. According to Psalm 139:13, God knows us and covers us in the womb of our mothers.[320] He knows the intricate details of our lives because He knits every detail together. He has a plan for our lives to do good toward us and not evil.[321] Death is not the end plan for God's people. He came that mankind would have life and a quality of life.[322]

The Supremacy of God vs. The Supreme Court

On January 22, 1973, Roe v. Wade became the landmark decision of the United States Supreme Court which ruled that the United States Constitution protects a pregnant woman's choice to have an abortion.[323] A fundamental "right to privacy," intrinsic in the Due Process Clause of the Fourteenth Amendment, was ruled to protect this choice.[324] The court ruled that a woman can have an abortion without excessive government restrictions. Such statement suggests that the government can provide safety guidelines for abortion to protect women's health without deciding for her if she can have an elective abortion.

Battle lines became less blurred during the 2020 elections. However, Americans still do not have 20/20 vision on one of the most debated and pressing issues prior to the election. The topic was placed on the backburner while Americans turned their attention to debates and fights regarding mask wearing, social distancing, discrimination against and attacks on Asian Americans, and other persisting problems. The discussion of abortion is but one expansive topic under women's rights. It is deeper than the right to have an abortion. The discussion also includes who will pay for abortions. As with contraceptives, some argue that such procedures and methods of birth control should not be covered by insurance. The debate becomes more inflamed by the consideration of rape victims and adolescents who are not mature enough to parent. Unfortunately, the legal debate over abortion is a very political one. The Pledge of Allegiance to the flag states "one nation under God." The Declaration of Independence refers to God as Nature's God and Creator. The Constitution of the United States does not refer to God as such. Hence, some ambiguity surfaces with the interpretation of the archival documents and the law itself. Politicians tend to turn and twist the debate in the direction which feeds them more votes and supporters at the polls. The question arises, "Is the debate or platform one way or the other regarding abortion and same-sex marriage a political ploy of some candidates to win votes, or do the candidates really have a moral stance on the issues?" Some candidates would argue that they are in favor of the democracy and a person's right to choose.

Whatever the Supreme Court rules or whatever candidates build their platforms upon, the Supremacy of God will still prevail. This does not mean that those who hold fast to God's Word will always see legislation in favor of the Bible. It definitely means that God is supreme and the final authority. Amazingly, Christians are split on the issue of abortion. Many feel that it is absolutely wrong no matter the situation. Some Christians believe that it is situational and based upon circumstances such as rape, molestation, and medical reasons. While the courts and even the churches go on debating the issue, God has already decided. The prophet Isaiah reinforces this position with the following statement, "Thus saith the Lord, thy redeemer, and he that formed thee from the womb, I am the Lord that maketh all things; that stretcheth forth the heavens along; that spreadeth abroad the earth by myself."[325] Human beings live in the mind of God before the thought of a child is ever conceived in the mind or the womb of a mother. God sets His anointed apart before birth by His grace.[326] Before a child is ever formed in the womb, God knows him. Life begins with the giver of life, God Himself. Jesus is the truth and the life and the only way to God the Father.[327] Since life begins with God, life begins with His very thoughts of a child before he or she ever enters the womb. This is the supremacy of God. Life is not dictated by the formation of organ systems or the aggregation of cell. Neither is it dictated by a certain amount days after a conception or a sexual encounter.

Pro-life vs. Pro-birth

Americans are being defined more and more by labels. In many cases, these categorizations only serve to widen the gap among

Americans within protected classes. A differentiation has already been determined between pro-choice and pro-life. However, there is another distinct difference necessary to explore between pro-life and pro-birth. Sister Joan Chittister, a Benedictine nun, is quoted by The Odyssey Online for her perspective of the two:

> "I do not believe that just because you're opposed to abortion, that that makes you pro-life. In fact, I think in many cases, your morality is deeply lacking if all you want is a child born but not a child fed, not a child educated, not a child housed. And why would I think that you don't? Because you don't want any tax money to go there. That's not pro-life. That's pro-birth. We need a much broader conversation on what the morality of pro-life is."[328]

This statement is one tossed to and fro. Cultural relativism leaps into the discussion from several angles. For many African Americans, the pro-life agenda is really a pro-birth agenda hiding under its heading. Pro-birth is a reference to the idea that people are more concerned with not killing babies but are not progressively concerned about providing essential things for life according to Maslow's hierarchy of needs. For many African Americans, this is the resemblance of slavery. African Americans were considered property and like livestock; and yet, endured some of the harshest treatment and living conditions. With the Emancipation Proclamation of January 1, 1863 and the Juneteenth Independence Day of June 19, 1865, African Americans were "said" free, but many did not feel set free because of the lack of economic support and educational opportunity which characterized systemic racism. Beyond 1865, African Americans continued to experience difficulties in American history. African Americans were granted citizenship in 1868 by the Fourteenth Amendment of the Constitution. The Civil Rights Act of 1964 outlawed discrimination based on race, color, religion, sex, or national origin. The 1965

Voting Rights Act, which prohibited the states from using literacy tests and other methods of exclusion from voting, changed the status of African Americans throughout the South.[329] At least one hundred years post emancipation, African Americans experienced hardships for lack of avenues and resources readily available for life enhancement. These findings are evidenced by the desegregation of schools and armed forces.

Woefully, Americans remain segregated on issues of morality and much of the divide is based on the poor past practices and historical calamites of the past. Many minorities assert that pro-lifers are really pro-birth. With the end of slavery, how can this argument be plausible? In 2019 as Americans anticipated the upcoming 2020 elections in the midst of a global pandemic, they waded in wonder of what the optics would be concerning racism, racial disparities in healthcare, abortions, and discrimination toward the LGBTQIAPK community. For the future, will America see through the dark glass of the past 200-year history, or will she see through the lenses of God's Word? Perhaps the real need for American Christians is to consider the reflection produced by looking into the mirror of the Word. The desired reflection should be of an individual who seeks justice, loves kindness, and walks humbly with God.[330] Christians are to learn to do good, correct oppression, bring justice to the fatherless, and plead the widow's cause.[331] The cry of many pro-choice individuals is that the pro-lifers do not care for children who are abused or hungry and for mothers who endure the same. Pro-lifers argue that their support of full-term pregnancy is evident in parenting support programs and adoption programs. Many conservative pro-lifers assert that they vote conservatively because of the waste of government funds for contraceptives and abortions. Americans should stop viewing the issue through partisan lenses. Planned Parenthood, which is funded by the government, has earned millions of government dollars to fund its programs. It is alleged that the organization jeopardizes the health and safety of women and girls by abetting the sex trafficking of minor girls.[332] Americans cannot simply show up to the polls as

Democrats and Republicans to vote on this and other challenging issues. Instead, Americans who are Christians must show up to the polls to vote the issue. If Christians would cross the bipartisan aisle which divides Americans, serious conversation can ensue. The government funding which goes toward Planned Parenthood and the cost for abortion providers can be used for human trafficking rehabilitation programs, foster care, and parenting programs. Have we thought about defunding such programs to help the living to thrive?

Abortion vs. Death Row

The political unrest in America is the result of the lack of God's love. Isaiah 49:15 (KJV) says, "Can a woman forget her sucking child, that she should not have compassion on the son her of womb? Yea, they may forget, yet will I not forget thee."[333] God loves people so much that He sent His Son to die for all to be saved. The church has a responsibility to be extenders of His love and grace. A lack of love, whether at birth or beyond, has the potential to end deadly. Christians must demonstrate the enduring love of God for those who are unborn and those who are serving on death row. Some Americans comment that crime could possibly be controlled by aborting babies who will be subject to rejection, abuse, and poor living conditions. Certainly, these things contribute to the emotional and mental instability of individuals, especially those who commit crimes. Other Americans push for capital punishment of those who commit certain crimes. Even with the ever-increasing number of wrongfully accused people on death row discovered with the forensic value of DNA testing, some Americans still support capital punishment but call themselves pro-life. The topic of social injustice is brewing on the Bunsen burner of killings of African Americans in the United States without justice. Memorial Day of 2020 will definitely be most memorable in the history of this country. The world watched for 9 minutes and 29 seconds as a Minnesota police officer placed his knee on the neck of an African American man lying on the ground unable to move and begging for his mother. Mr. George Floyd uttered the words of many before him who died at the knee or hand of police officers, "I can't breathe." Prior to Mr. Floyd's death, Mr. Ahmaud Arbery was out for a run in his community and never made it back home. Mr. Arbery was chased down and killed by armed Caucasian residents in his South Georgia neighborhood. I would not otherwise mention race descriptions in my writings. For the sake of discussion and portrayal of the climate in America at the time of this penning, it is important that I mention these specifics. Now, please stay with me here. Approximately seven years prior to this writing, I took a great interest in the number of abortions happening in the state of Louisiana. The data was overwhelming for me so I decided to educate the community regarding the numbers. We opened our hearts and our doors to men and women who had experienced abortion. The event was called, "Unborn Lives Matter." It was definitely a night of healing. From 2014-2019, the number of abortions in the state of Louisiana fell 20 percent.[334] The 2019 statistics for Louisiana reveal that 8,144 abortions were reported. Among black women, 5,142 abortions were reported.[335] Among white women, 2,148 abortions were performed.[336] In both categories, the greatest number of abortions by women 25-29 years old.[337] Data also proved that the highest number of abortions were among unmarried women. Looking at the data, reported abortions among black and white women, not inclusive of other groups, revealed a 58% higher rate among black women. Louisiana is just one state with these daunting numbers. Why are these discussions so important and relevant to one another? These are important discussions when we consider the persistence or future of African Americans. What are the root causes that lead women to consider abortions as an option? Do the numbers reflect the disparities that exist between racial groups in America? There is much chatter regarding "black on black" crime in contest of the protests against the injustice of African

Americans at the hand of police officers. I should assert here, that same color or same race crime occurs among all racial groups. As an African American woman, I chose to speak here regarding African Americans, especially considering recent events. It is my strong belief that we must afford all these matters appropriate attention within their space. All too often, one of these is used to counter the discussion of the other. They all must be given due diligence and separate attention for the holistic health of the people who are affected by them.

As it relates to the pro-life discussion, how can we consider someone pro-life who does not have a problem with the existing disparities among living people? How can pro-lifers be okay with anyone being wrongfully accused of a crime, serving death row for a wrongfully accused crime, and/or spending years in prison for the same? How can a pro-life contender turn and look in the opposite direction when unjust sentences are handed down to some groups of people while others serve little or no time for the same crime or infraction? Did not the writer of Hebrews say to remember them that are in bonds, as bound with them; and them which suffer adversity, as being yourselves also in the body?[338] According to Matthew 25:36 believers are to clothe the naked and visit those in prison.[339] The brewing debate over differing political stances on abortion and death row can be resolved with the resolute heart to obey God's commandments to take care of widows, orphans, and visit the prisoner. If we provide resources to train up a child in the way of the Lord, we will see a decline in crimes committed.[340]

The Christian Responsibility in Abortion

A little leaven leavens the whole lump.[341] Christians cannot float carefree in the lukewarm waters of indifference. A little bit of false teaching or compromise of God's Word results in our whole lives being negatively affected. Whether one chooses to see abortion as a legal or a moral issue, or both, one must definitely understand that it is sin. Still births, the health of a mother, and other medical dangers which compromise the health of a mother are still being debated by members of the church. Mothers stricken with the decision to consume toxic drugs for treatment of cancer while pregnant have a tough decision to make. Unlike same-sex marriage partners and some members of the LGBTQIAPK community, women who have had abortions have not done so for the sake of its non-existent pleasure. Members of the LGBTQIAPK community seek the opportunity to be free outwardly, while women who have had abortions struggle with being free to speak about it.

The church has a great responsibility in both the hinderance and healing of women who have had abortions. The scripture is clear that God wants His people to seek His face, humble themselves, repent, and pray and He will heal their land.[342] Before the church can stand in the world, she must bow humbly in prayer and repentance while seeking God's direction and His favor. Regardless of the law of the land, some women's feelings toward having abortions will not change. However, the Word of God *can* change those feelings. Unfortunately, many of the abortions that have happened are unconfessed. Guttmacher has quoted that approximately 40% of women surveyed post abortion indicated they are Protestant Christians with more than half being Catholic.[343] Care Net, a Life Way Research sponsor, surveyed 1,038 women regarding having an abortion and their views on church.[344] When polled, 33% of women considered their abortions decision based on the expectation they would be judged and another 26% based on condemnation.[345] Out of the women surveyed, only 7% would speak to someone at a local church, 7% would speak to a pregnancy care center worker, and 10% would speak to a counselor.[346] The survey indicated that 43% of women who have had an abortion agree that it is safe to talk with a pastor about abortion.[347] Sadly, 49% of women who have had an abortion agree that pastors' teachings on forgiveness do not seem to apply to terminated pregnancies and 39% agree that pastors are sensitive to the pressures a woman faces with an unplanned pregnancy.[348]

The church must begin asking herself the right questions about abortion. For starters, the church needs to get off the fence regarding the sin. Furthermore, women need to feel secure that the church is a safe place for confession. Gossip, condemnation, and judgment all compromise the effectiveness of counseling. Christian counselors and pastors should counsel in confidentiality. In an interview with a woman who had an abortion, Christine Hoover recorded the anonymous interviewee's statement, "Shame thrives in secrecy."[349] If women are going to experience the light of God's Word, they cannot continue to settle in the darkness of unconfessed secrets. The murder and resulting void leave the woman pregnant with shame. According to the survey, pastors need to work at being more open and sensitive regarding women dealing with post-abortion grief. The church does not have to be acceptive of the sin of abortion to be receptive of the woman. In many cases, the church needs to repent for judging and failing to be a trusted place of refuge for those struggling with sin.

Some women may have abortions because of their affiliation with a church and/or their membership in prominent families. Fear of embarrassment and being humiliated may make confession as difficult as having been pregnant. Other women are forced by their partner to abort. No matter the reason, the church cannot opt out of the opportunity to help with the healing, confession, and forgiveness process. David Powlison suggests that women who have had abortions should heal by praying aloud their confession.[350] Powlison believes that it is good for the counselee to be able to acknowledge her sin and take seriously what is wrong. Open confession helps the counselee to move past the guilt. Reassurance that God loves and forgives will help the counselee to get over the shame. Counseling women who have had abortion can help to prevent multiple abortions. Open dialogue and biblical discussions regarding sex and abortion should be offered in the Christian education offerings of churches. Schools teach sex education, but do not talk about abstinence from a biblical perspective. Pastors, Christian leaders, Christian counselors, and parents should work to equip the younger generations with God's Word and His desire that all who will receive Jesus will have everlasting life. Many women suffer with the silence of abortion, because of the obvious display of physical changes which accompany pregnancy. Rather than to embrace the development of a growing child within, many women suffer from a gaping hole in their emotional and spiritual integrity. Biblical counseling which acknowledges abortion as sin but compassionately leads the counselee to repentance is the pathway to restoration.

CHAPTER 10

THE PROBLEM: NATURAL REPRODUCTIVE LOSS

Why does it matter if two people of the same-sex desire to marry? Why not allow a woman to decide when or if she wants to be a mother and allow her body to go through changes? Who says an individual decision cannot be made regarding the use of contraceptives? These are just a few pondered questions related to challenging topics of contemporary times. Again, Christian counselors must prepare to answer these questions from a biblical perspective. While the topics may present differing challenges, the problems are all answered by one source, the Word of God. Genesis 1:28 (KJV) says, "And God blessed them, and God said unto them, Be fruitful, and multiply, and replenish the earth, and subdue it: and have dominion over the fish of the sea, and over the fowl of the air, and over every living thing that moveth upon the earth." Genesis 22:17 (KJV) says, "That in blessing I will bless thee, and in multiplying thy seed as the stars of the heaven, and as the sand which is upon the sea shore; and thy seed shall possess the gate of his enemies." From these two scriptures, God's intent for man to multiply is evident and concise. Clearly, whatever goes against the will of God is sin. The book of Genesis is pregnant with the potential of generations to come. God established families and blessed them for the ongoing production of mankind. Are we procreative if we sit quietly while abortions are being performed and same-sex marriages continue? In Genesis 38:9–10, Onan spilled his seed on the ground after having relations with his brother's wife because he did not wish to bear a son to her that was not his.[351] This displeased God and He slew Onan for his disobedience. Onan fulfilled the desire of his flesh but did not produce the will of God. Man is still fulfilling the desires of his flesh void of the will of God. Pornography, sexually explicit material whether printed or visual material, is spreading rapidly due to the increasing presence of internet in daily use. Psychology Today reports that the world's largest pornography site claims that in 2018, it had a daily average of 92 million unique viewers with the great majority of them male.[352] Pornography has been known to be connected to sexual uncertainty in adolescents.[353] The Journal of Women's Health reports that 83% of adult heterosexual women have viewed pornography; however, less than 43.5% use it for masturbation.[354] The subject of masturbation is often overlooked by Christians. Some say it is sinful to engage in while others think it is healthy and prevents the engagement of *other* activities. Self-gratification is not the purposed sex model God created for husband and wife. A person is not designed to engage "self." God created Eve for Adam. He said that it is not good for man to live alone.[355] With the increase in pornography, there is also an increase in sex trafficking and divorce.

Families are being destroyed by the constant onslaught of distractions from the internet, social media, television, radio, and other media which promote messages that do not support the wholesomeness of family life. The breakdown of the family is Satan's tool to tear apart the kingdom of God and prevent it from multiplying. Abortions obviously decrease the number of children being born each year. Same-sex marriages and other same-sex relationships among LGBTQIAPK community members decrease the number of births. These couples are considering other avenues for starting families in addition to adoption. Among the other avenues are methods of assisted reproductive technology, which allows at least one member of the couple to be related genetically to the child and surrogate. These methods are even used among heterosexual couples who may be struggling with conceiving. More babies are being born by induced labor. Mothers are often scheduled for induced labor as if they were being scheduled for caesarean sections.

Is there anything natural anymore? Do these methods remove God from the picture? Are miracles being narrowed down to pitre dishes, injections, and calendar dates? Couples contemplating use of assisted reproduction technology, may contend that God has given scientists the intellect to produce little miracles from these forms of technology. Is adoption counseling offered enough within the church? While traditional medicine offers expensive methods that may or may not work, should some couples or individuals consider adoption as a biblical choice to take care of the orphan? I am reminded of a time that I sat in the passenger seat as my sister, Leigh, drove along while the falling rain danced along the street. I had been quieted back into my seat by the pitter patter of the dancing rain. As we approached a red light, we slowed down long enough for me to make a unique observation. I took note of the water sprinklers going at full blast in the yard of a lovely home nearby. Just to clarify, I broke the silence in the car and asked Leigh if she had taken note of the functioning sprinklers. Having confirmed that the sprinklers were going at full blast, I remember being in awe of what I'd witnessed. Now remember that it was raining, yet the sprinkler system was at full blast. Before, I could judge the homeowners for wasting water in the rain, God spoke clearly to me. He said, "This is what it looks like when you try to help Me." What a humbling moment. Many of us try to manufacture miracles at one time or another rather than trusting that God knows what we need. We need to seek Him first. Perhaps that homeowner didn't believe that the forecasted rain would be enough to take care of a dry situation. I don't know. However, I do know that God does all things well.

Although we are not control of many things, there are some

things that we must remain abreast of such as current events, medical developments, and other issues which may affect the livelihood of individuals challenged by these tough decisions. When it became available, parents pondered over the thought of allowing their sons and daughters to be injected with Gardasil, a vaccination for human papillomavirus, HPV. The vaccination, which is used for the prevention of cancers caused by the disease, is recommended for boys and girls ages 11-12.[356] Much debate arose over the injection of young boys and girls at such young ages for the prevention of a *sexually* transmitted disease. Moral and cultural relativism won the debate. Many parents refused to vaccinate their children fearing that to do so would send the message to the child that unprotected sex or sex at all would be okay. Many pediatricians learned how to share the need for the vaccination to children and parents by simply educating the child that by receiving the vaccination early he or she will have a reduced chance of getting cancer later. Medical doctors learned to place *less* emphasis on HPV as being a *sexually* transmitted disease and began focusing on educating parents on the vaccination's ability to prevent cancer.

Christian counselors should urge couples to pray about tough decisions. Non-traditional couples should be given guidance from the Word of God without compromise to its stance on marriage and family. In the case of parents, counselors should rely upon the Bible and other Christian resources in various professions to assist with answering questions and gaining insight and understanding. Unfortunately, much is still to be learned and decided upon regarding the use of contraceptives for treatment of women's health issues such as endometriosis, fibroid complications, and menorrhagia. Many insurance companies, employers, and taxpayers feel that contraceptives should not be a covered expense. Viagra, sildenafil citrate, is a prescription medicine used to treat erectile dysfunction.[357] In this regard, the medicine may be considered as a drug for pleasure and recreation. However, this same drug is used for the treatment of pulmonary hypertension, a disease which can be very debilitating if left untreated.[358] If insurance companies opt not to pay for the drug because of its use for erectile dysfunction, several patients would not be able to afford the drug therapy leaving them to suffer from the complications of pulmonary hypertension. Women suffering from fibroid tumors, menorrhagia, and endometriosis will also find themselves suffering both physical pain *and* financial burden as a result of not being able to afford birth control pills or other contraceptives used in the treatment of these diseases. Will birth control be coded by insurance companies as estrogen hormone therapy for the disease or will it be coded as a contraceptive? The dual use and sometimes even the multiple use of these drugs for treating various diseases may result in the progression of disease processes, rather than in the prevention of them. This duality is not limited to the drug's ability to treat the patient, but this duality has also resulted in a "duel" between members of Congress, pharmaceutical companies, and Americans. How can insurance companies prove that physicians are prescribing these medications for the benefit of treating life-threatening or life-limiting diseases? Who determines what a life-threatening or life-limiting disease is? The questions only provoke answers that will place Americans in another category for which they will have to meet the criteria for. Pharmaceutical companies and insurance companies are not the only groups "duking" it out over these types of issues while Americans linger in limbo for an answer. The legalization of marijuana is another hot topic for discussion. Many Americans argue against the arrest and outrageous prison sentences handed down to those convicted of selling marijuana illegally. Starting a legal business requires that the necessary documents be filed as required by each state and the federal government. Hence, the argument for street-sell of marijuana is nullified. However, the charges applied for selling are debatable. Marijuana is a drug that serves well those who suffer great pain and are known to be terminally ill. However, illegal use of the drug cannot be justified by the drug's legalization.

For Christian counselors and other Christian leaders, the answers will not be cookie cutter for these and many other contemporary issues. Counselors must hold fast to the truth of God's Word. While these issues may be considered contemporary for church leaders, they are not new to God. Within their scope of time, human beings have always dealt with the dilemma of the day as if it were the worst thing that ever happened in history. Nevertheless, God is, has been, and will be consistent throughout history.

CHAPTER 11

ARTIFICIAL INTELLIGENCE

We have discussed natural reproduction, but what about spiritual reproduction? Is the church reproducing after God or after the flesh? The world has its agenda. However, the church is in the world but not of the world; yet there seems to be a decreasing gap between the world and the church while the gap between God and the church seems to be widening. The holy scriptures speak of the apostasy and the great falling away.[359] We discussed the identity crisis in reference to the LGBTQIAPK community, but what about the faith crisis in the church? Religious "Nones" are a group of people, mainly millennials, who have decided not to identify with any religion.[360] "Dones" are Christians who are leaving the church but still believe in God.[361] Most "Dones" have worked in church but have decided to leave. Sociologists ponder the future of the church. Members of the Body of Christ are made in the image of God and should be producing as such. As mentioned in Chapter 6, John 14:12-14 speaks about the "greater works." Jesus encourages His disciples regarding the work of the kingdom. He tells them *they* will do greater works.[362] The key here is to ask in the name of Jesus and whatever you ask for in reference to the kingdom will be done. With the exodus of some members of the church, how will the greater works continue? Who's available and producing for God?

Theological or Technological

More churches are choosing to remain "connected" through social media outlets and websites. Efforts to remain relevant in the 21st Century have led to internet streaming of worship services. Rather than getting dressed and driving to a local church, some people opt to tune in from their bed, breakroom, or from a couch. Hebrews 10:25 (KJV) says, "Not forsaking the assembling of ourselves together, as the manner of some is; but exhorting one another: and so much the more, as ye see the day approaching." Does this mean that we must get dressed and drive to a local building to be with other Christians? Or did the writer of Hebrews say "assembling" because the church did not have internet at the time it was written? While the viewing or listening audience may be connected electronically and technologically, are they connected spiritually? How is a person baptized who only tunes in via internet or radio? Will the future of the church be to tune in from your personal space and treat the place of worship like a drive-thru for other needs?

How are real relationships birthed technologically? Families are growing further apart due to texting and social media. Individuals feel a need to be more connected with what is happening in the world or with friends rather than enjoying life with the family members who God has blessed them with. With increasing developments in technology, contemporary society continues its trend of labeling and categorizing individuals. Unfortunately, society defines an individual by his or her *function* or *profession*. Individuals who submit to the societal pressures of being and functioning in the box of someone else's expectation will suffer an identity crisis. Not only are people defined by what they do, but they are defined by what they possess as well. Some children and adults, alike, feel that they *must* have the latest cellular phone on the market. Being able to function in the world of the internet or artificial intelligence makes people feel accomplished and secure. On the contrary, what good would it do for us to gain the world and yet lose our souls?[363] Are we so busy with solving the problems of the world ourselves that we fail to pray to the Problem Solver of the universe?

As creations of God, made in His image, human beings possess a higher intellect than any other creature. It can be expected that human beings will do great things. Many great inventions and new discoveries appear increasingly. Among these are smart devices such as phones and watches which can control the security systems of our homes and offices while monitoring our heart rates at the same time. Have we considered how much stress and anxiety we introduce into our lives by being connected so often through these devices? Philippians 4:6 (KJV) says, "Be careful for nothing; but in every thing by prayer and supplication with thanksgiving let your requests be made known unto God." Fear and anxiety are big business. The evil duo has promoted the need for security systems, spyware, carnal weapons, and even pills. God has not given us the spirit of fear.[364] The more we allow ourselves to control our own safety and well-being through smart devices the less safe we really are. That's really not *spiritually* smart at all. The very tools designed to keep us safe such as home security camera systems are the very things that leave us vulnerable to invasion of our privacy by hackers. Our God definitely supplies us with wisdom; however, we must be wise enough not to place our trust in anything or anyone other than Him. When we depend more upon ourselves to control our lives and provide for our own well-being apart from Him, we risk becoming gods in our own eyes. With the latest scientific developments, some people question, "What is the need for God?"

Artificial Intelligence, Emotional Intelligence, & Social Intelligence

How intelligent is artificial intelligence if it is artificial? According to B. J. Copeland, artificial intelligence is the theory and development of computer systems able to perform tasks that normally require human intelligence, such a visual perception, speech recognition, decision-making, and translation between languages.[365] Robotics has expanded within various fields and been proven useful for surgery and even for more dangerous jobs like coal mining. Notwithstanding the benefits of artificial intelligence, there still are some concerns. The threat of job scarcity and human interaction is a reality. How emotionally intelligent are the devices that we use every day? Text messages and emails are examples of misinterpreted forms of communication due to the lack of human interaction.

Emotional intelligence is the capacity to be aware of, control, and express one's emotions, and to handle interpersonal relationships judiciously and empathetically.[366] Emotional intelligence allows us to be more self-aware; thereby, allowing us to be more in control of our own emotions. Social intelligence on the other hand is how we interact with others. Human beings have the ability to be socially and emotionally intelligent. However, robots and computers are incomparable to emotionally healthy human beings. Robots will not have the ability to auto correct themselves emotionally and socially. Attempting to type a text message can be slightly challenging when the phone insists on auto-correcting the intended message. Situational leadership teaches that we lead and respond based upon the situation or the circumstance. Emotionally and socially stable individuals do not operate based on algorithms. Instead, stable individuals can adjust their response based upon information, environment, and/ or circumstance.

In 1950, Alan Turing coined the Turing test, a way of determining the intelligence of a computer or machine.[367] No matter the percentage at which a machine or computer meets or supersedes criteria of the Turing test, it will never be able to comprehend God. Robots and other machinery do not have a soul or spirit, and man does not have the ability to create these. The fact that man continues with attempts to make computers as intelligent as humans or more, speaks to the problem of pride and hidden narcissism in society. No one could or can ever compare with God. God allows human beings to reproduce after their own kind. Man's attempt to make computers intelligent as humans is an attempt at being as creative as the Creator, God. Such suggests that the Creator is equal to the creature. Left unchecked and out of control, artificial intelligence introduces the idea of transhumanism. Transhumanism is the belief or theory that humanity can evolve beyond its current physical and mental limitations, especially by means of science and technology.[368] Those who subscribe to this belief fall under a category labeled as transhumanists.

Gucci's "Cyborg" fashion show March 2018 sparked some commentary regarding transhumanism. Head designer Alessandro Michele said, "We are the Dr. Frankenstein of our lives...We exist to reproduce ourselves, but we have moved on. We are in the posthuman era, for sure, it is under way."[369] Vogue referred to the fashion show as transhuman in nature.[370] As with our discussion regarding transgender individuals and other members of the LGBTQIAPK community, transhumanists also may suffer an underlying identity issue. Transhumanism is the idea that human beings can live forever. Efforts are already in motion toward mapping the human brain and exploring methods of making individuals more intelligent. These efforts are seen as ways to extend life and prevent death. Man cannot live forever in his current state. The fashion industry has moved beyond growing old gracefully to not growing old at all. In the process, are better lives being created or are monsters being fashioned? Man's attempt to recreate himself or to alter God's purpose is futile.

Bill Joy, a chief scientist at Sun Microsystems, warned that self-replicating robots and advances in nanotechnology could be witnessed as early as 2030.[371] Theologians and scientists continue to debate what the essence of "created in His image" really means. Noreen Herzfeld explains that one goal of artificial intelligence is to create an "other in the image of God."[372] Yes, other. One interpretation of "created in His image" suggest that *function* is the key component.[373] If "function" is indeed the meaning of being created in the image of God, man would lack in the image of God. Stay with me. God has given us authority in the earth; however, human minds are finite and will never be able to comprehend the infinite wisdom of God. Many theologians and supporters of artificial intelligence, AI, agree that God has given dominion to man to exercise and that this dominion supports the idea that man has the authority to serve as God's deputy on earth.[374] However, the Old Testament also records that kings who went against the will of God invoked His wrath. Man's goal should never be to mirror God in power. A man who is aware of his own deficits and weaknesses will be more likely to depend on God. In man's weakness, God's strength is made perfect for him.[375]

When the Eugene, a Russian-designed chatbot, passed the Turing test, the world of computer programmers celebrated a great breakthrough in technology. However, passing the Turing test met man's standard and not God's. Kate Levchuk wrote,

> "Our ability to create a soul in silico will be a litmus test for thousands of years of religious preachings, beliefs of millions of people and the strength of the biggest human institution- the Church. It would be an ultimate and undisputable triumph of Scientific Revolution. Equally, belief in the higher spirit will be strengthened if AGI turns out to be a programmer's fantasy."[376]

Why would man seek to create a soul? Man must understand that *our souls are not comparable with our intellect.* The soul is the spiritual connecting part of us that is given to God in our worship of Him in spirit and in truth. Man's attempt at creating the soul is foolhardy. No matter how intelligent man becomes artificially, it will never compare with God's creative power. Man's greatest intellectual production will be like having a form of godliness that denies the power thereof. Robots will never possess the heart of God or a soul.

Come Make Us gods...

Just how intelligent are human beings? Are there limitations for intelligent beings? Man's intellect often leads beyond safe borders into the terrain of pride and narcissism. These characteristics result in the need to control and to do in excess. Those who act upon these character flaws are often known to recreate themselves or take extreme pride in what they do. This is similar to the way the society identifies a person by their function or profession rather than by the content of their character. There are many instances where man creates a mess of things in the process of trying to recreate what he lusts after. Proverbs 3:5–6 (KJV) says, "Trust in the Lord with all thine heart; lean not to thine own understanding. In all thy ways acknowledge him and he will direct thy paths." With every path we must take, we should invoke the wisdom of God. Whether we are dealing with something artificially, emotionally, or socially, we need the guidance of God in our decision-making. Machines and computers do not have the capacity to decipher morality or to pray to God for guidance.

Man has always tried success apart from God only to have to find his way back to the loving arms of God. Joshua 1:7–9 (KJV) says,

> "Only be thou strong and very courageous, that they mayest observe to do according to all the law which Moses my servant commanded thee: turn not from it to the right hand or to the left, that thou mayest prosper whithersoever thou goest. This book of the law shall not depart out of thy mouth; but thou shalt meditate therein day and night, that thou mayest observe to do according to all that is written therein: for then thou shalt make their way prosperous, and then thou shalt have good success. Have not I commanded thee? Be strong

and of a good courage; be not afraid, neither be
thou dismayed: for the Lord thy God is with thee
whithersoever thou goest."

Here, the Lord reassures Joshua of how success comes. The lesson for Joshua is multifaceted. First, we are to be strong and courageous. The Lord reiterated this to Joshua. The enemy will create a smokescreen leading us to think we are well when we are not and that we should fear when we should not. At that time, the book of the law was all Joshua had, so God told him to meditate on the Word and not to stray away from it to the left or the right. If we are to have true success in life, we do not have to pursue it; instead, we must pursue God and live in His Word. Our pursuit is the kingdom of God and His righteousness.[377] Often, we find ourselves moving left or right because of fear, pride, or other reasons which contradict God's command. Joshua was following Moses in leadership. Early on, God instructs him to lean on the book of the law. What does this mean for contemporary Christians? We, too, must remain steadfast in the faith. It is not necessary to recreate the wheel or the will of God. When we do, we provoke the wrath of God.

In Chapter 32 of the Book of Exodus, it is evident what happens when man becomes inpatient and fails to trust God's process. The people were inpatient when Moses did not return from the mount at the time of *their* expectation. They decided to take matters into their own hands. Exodus 32:1 (KJV) reads, "And when the people saw that Moses delayed to come down out of the mount, the people gathered themselves together unto Aaron, and said unto him, Up, make us gods, which shall go before us; for as for this Moses, the man that brought us up out of the land of Egypt, we wot not what is become of him." Aaron made the mistake of telling the people to break off the earrings of their wives, sons, and daughters to bring to him. Once he gathered all the earrings, he fashioned a golden calf. The people responded by saying, "These be thy gods, O Israel, which brought thee up out of the land of Egypt."[378] The people began to worship what had been made from human hands. They attributed glory to a golden calf rather than onto a loving God. Their hearts were still rooted in the love for their gods in Egypt. Christian counselors have to beware of people like this. Some people will call upon the name of Jesus only when they are desperate and have no other option. Many will praise Him for the moment forgetting about Him for a lifetime. Counselors cannot assume just because someone is in the crowd led by a Christian leader that that individual is a Christian. It is important to verify an authentic relationship with the Lord. Many Christian leaders have probably questioned Aaron's motives. However, we have to consider how many times we may have compromised on doing what is right. Aaron compromised. In verse 5, Aaron built an altar before the golden calf and called for a feast unto the Lord.[379] Wait a minute. How are they going to have a feast unto the Lord and yet bring this engravened image to the altar? Aaron made the mistake of thinking that he could mix the worship of God the Father with the gods of Egypt. When we compromise on the Word of God, we commit the same sin as did Aaron. In Exodus 20:3–5 (KJV) God says,

> "Thou shalt have no other gods before me. Thou shalt not make unto thee any graven image, or any likeness of any thing that is in heaven above, or that is in the earth beneath, or that is in the water under the earth: Thou shalt not bow down thyself to them, nor serve them: for I the Lord thy God am a jealous God, visiting the iniquity of the fathers upon the children unto the third and fourth generation of them that hate me;"

Without doubt, Aaron went against the will of God. Many of counseling sessions and worship services have "golden calves" mixed into them. When we compromise God's commandments, we compromise deliverance and breakthrough. The lack of patience leads to destruction. M. T. Bass says, "Impatience is the cardinal sin of youth."[380] I say that impatience is the cardinal sin of the immature. How immature it is for man to be impatient with God and expect Him to be tolerant with human folly. The people were so self-centered and tried to have their cake and eat it too. Exodus 32:6 (KJV) says, "And they rose up early on the morrow, and offered burnt offerings, and brought peace offerings; and the people sat down to eat and to drink, and rose up to play." They had the audacity to worship the god that Aaron had made. As evidenced by their behavior, they did not take His command seriously. They went on playing and partying as if to celebrate what they had done. This behavior infuriated God. As a result, He sought to destroy them. Are we as dumb as our gods? The gods we create are lifeless, mute, and even with eyes and ears they are blind and deaf. When there are those who are faithful and uncompromising, God will spare. Moses was angry when he saw the people dancing around naked and partying as if they were still in Egypt. Chapter 32 of the Book of Exodus reveals what happens when a person seemingly moves away from the problem. Physical proximity and distance are not the only factors to consider. Without the proper evangelism to lead the person to salvation, it will not be long before that person returns to his own folly. Counselors cannot be fooled by counselees just because they attend counseling and seemingly have moved on from their problem. This trend is often witnessed in domestic abuse and drug addiction. When we are patient with God, we are renewed and strengthened. Afterall, God is patient with us. Humanity weakens when we depend more on the latest GPS system rather than depending on the guidance of the Holy Spirit. All too often, we place our trust in manmade devices and those who have positions of power rather than trusting the Lord.

Let Us Build Us a City and a Tower...

Every human victory should be accompanied by intentional praise and glory to God. When man fails to give God glory, man risks becoming narcissistic and independent of God. Again, society has forced human beings to be categorized into groups and labeled by anything from profession, diet, size, sexual preference, and the list continues. Without these categories and labels, human beings are diverse enough simply based upon born characteristics. Yet, we seek to be more different rather than to celebrate those things we share. No wonder philosophers spend so much time studying cultural and moral relativism, and moral pluralism. Because of our quest for diversification, we must consider that cultural mannerisms and linguistical meanings of things are different for varying groups.

Apparent from the beginning, God desires that His people be communicable with and in fellowship with one another. Early on the whole earth was of one language, and of one speech. The need to be different and set apart has been a human desire from the beginning. The children of men found a plain in the land of Shinar and decided to make brick and mortar as material to build their own city and tower.[381] Genesis 11:4–5 (KJV) says, "And they said, Go to, let us build us a city and a tower, whose top may reach unto heaven; and let us make us a name, lest we be scattered abroad upon the face of the whole earth. And the Lord came down to see the city and the tower, which the children of men builded." The grammar in verse 6 is especially important to its meaning. "And the Lord said, Behold, the people is one, and they have all one language; and this they begin to do: and now nothing will be restrained from them, which they have imagined to do."[382] The text reads that the *people is* one rather than the *people are* one. Clearly, the meaning and intent is that God desired that people be as one corporate unit rather than subgroups of people. In our worship of God, He desires the voice of one though there may be many. The grammar in verse 7 is important as well. God says, "Go to, let *us* go down, and there confound their language, that they may not understand one another's speech." (emphasis mine) This reference to "us" is not of a plural God, but instead of a Triune God present in the beginning.

When the people sought to separate themselves and build their city and tower to the heavens, God confused their language and scattered them abroad and they left off to build the city. God let it be so and confounded their language, calling the place Babel. Even in contemporary times, man is content to separate himself from his fellow brother but is not willing to sanctify himself unto God. In our hands are little compact devices which can take us around the world while sitting home in our living rooms. These same devices can also take us away from our families. With social media and other distractions, many are distracted with knowing the latest news or trying to meet the expectations of others while competing with the rest. It is becoming rarer for families to sit and talk without a mobile or cellular device which keeps them connected to the outside world. While the children of men built their own city and tower in Genesis 11, men of the 21st century are building cellphone towers and other inventions. Unfortunately, breakthroughs in technology are ruining human interaction. Don't get me wrong. With the onslaught of COVID-19 around the world, many of us were forced to quarantining and social distancing. With these measures in place, we have had to learn how to use technology to continue preaching, teaching, providing telehealth, shopping, and doing much more. However, we still must have an equilibrium which affords us human interaction.

Christian leaders and counselors should remain ever knowledgeable about the use of devices. 2 Corinthians 2:11 (KJV) says, "Lest Satan should get an advantage of us: for we are not ignorant of his devices." Often, affairs and neglect of our human interactions are the result of addictions to devices. Much of the anxiety, trauma, and stress counselees experience is connected to the subtle messages from social networks. Pornography sites, dating sites, and other avenues have made adultery easier to commit right from the palm of our hands. Christian leaders and counselors must endeavor to teach others how to remain grounded in God and planted in Him in times of major technological advancements. Often, we see these advancements as blessings, making our daily lives a little less hectic. However, we should always consider if these advancements in technology result in complications and compromise of our theology.

CHAPTER 12

THE CONCLUSION TO A NEW BEGINNING

Jesus Christ is the answer for the world. Every problem or issue can find its resolve in the Word of God. The Word of God is the only answer that is universal, absolute, and resolute. Other methods are not comprehensive solutions to problems and issues discussed here. The Word of God is universal because it is indiscriminate and applicable to all. Jesus' sacrifice at Calvary bridged the gap between God and mankind and between Jews and Gentiles. The Word of God is absolute because it is without error. It is indisputable. Philosophy, psychology, theory, and law all leap from the springboard of the Word of God. None of these have its own rudimentary beginnings. Each argument stems from agreement or disagreement with the Word. Nevertheless, it (the Word) is the foundation of all times. Even when we do not receive our desired answer, the Word stands in every situation.

Christian counselors must submit wholeheartedly to the Holy Spirit's guidance, adhere to the Word of God, and commit to compassion without compromise. Christian counselors must be Christians who counsel rather than counselors who happen to be Christians. The work requires astuteness to God's Word and a discerning spirit. Possessing morals is not enough. Counselors should assess what moral value means relatively and culturally to the counselee. Assumption should not be a part of the equation by which conclusion regarding morality is reached. It is imperative, particularly in the hour in which we counsel and minister to the masses, that we introduce the kingdom culture to counselees. Its morals are based on the absolute Word of God and not the opinions, preferences, and idealistic distortions of man. So many people wish to pick and choose which religious principle they will follow and practice. Some desire not to own any religious beliefs at all. Hence, moral relativism is not reliable.

Love has to be the leading force when counseling. Both compassion and an uncompromising strategy are rooted in love. Paul said, "Am I therefore your enemy, because I tell you the truth?"[383] If we love our fellow man, we will not compromise on the truth of God's word to either appease ourselves or anyone else. Love is sacrificial. Sacrificial love is not self-serving. Christian counseling is Christ-centered, and its goal is to bring the counselee to the point of pleasing Christ, rather than others or self. Pleasing self is a destructive nature. Unfortunately, may authors and philosophers are teaching the importance of self without regard for God. The self-centeredness of mankind replaces absolutism with relativism. God's love is indescribable and indisputable. Christian counselors must apply truth through love. Ephesians 4:15 says (KJV), "But speaking the truth in love, may grow up into him in all things, which is the head, even Christ:"[384] Great balance must be practiced in the process of counseling. Therapy should never supersede theology. Instead, theology should guide therapy. Caution should be practiced even when applying theology. Some counselees suffer from the pathology of religion resulting in them striving for an unobtainable perfection and sometimes living self-righteously. Beginning counseling with an assessment of salvation is vital to for a successful outcome. Salvation is a critical slice in the larger scheme of counseling success. Evangelism is the counselors' primary objective in cases where the counselee is not sure of his salvation or where the counselee is an unbeliever.

There are few biblical topics worth exploring in counseling

for effectiveness. Grace, justification, and sanctification should be explained and or reviewed. Counselors must keep in mind that many counselees will have been baptized and will have attended church but would have never benefitted from an in-depth study and survey of these topics. If counseling is to be effective, it must be implemented without condemnation. Jesus' uncompromising love should always be at the center of counseling; therefore, condemnation is forbidden. Compassionate counseling focuses on the grace of God, leading the counselee to seek to please Him rather than "self" or anyone else. Counseling which integrates justification and sanctification meets both the immediate and progressive needs of the counselee. Justification deals with the immediate work of grace and faith in Jesus Christ. Sanctification deals with the on-going work of God's grace.

The presence and spiritual guidance of Christian counselors is necessary to meet the counseling needs of the 21st century. The world is becoming more and more diverse. With diversity comes subcategorization. God's intention is to have one body, the church, with diverse gifts. Man has distorted the original plan of God by making diversity about race, color, age, ethnicity, sex, gender, creed, and sexual orientation. From these categories, we see some of history's most disturbing events. Racism, skin color, age discrimination, class abuse, identity crisis, backsliding, and same-sex marriage are only a few of the issues being experienced because of subdivisions. God's Word calls for unity. It seems the world has sought ways to further divided itself and yet be accepted as separate. God has called for one separation. That separation is sanctification; whereby, we are to separate ourselves from the world and embrace Jesus as Lord. Diversity and inclusion seem like wonderful topics on the surface. A biblical analysis of these will demonstrate how much we are expected to compromise in order to be accepting. We can love and be considerate without the risk of compromise. America is no longer one nation under God. Instead, America is many subcategories under the relative choice of an individual. Globally and locally, our problems are not many things as we suppose them to be. Instead, they are summed to equal a lack of obedience to God. A nation not rooted in the principles thereof is predestined for calamity. Psalm 33:12 (KJV) says, "Blessed is the nation whose God is the Lord; and the people whom he hath chose for his own inheritance."[385] Proverbs 14:34 (KJV) says, "Righteousness exalteth a nation: but sin is a reproach to any people."[386] These two scriptures remind us of the importance of serving and submitting to God. When we compromise as a nation and as a people, we do not spare calamity. Politicians, alone, cannot be held liable for making decisions regarding our allegiance to God. While we may hold true our allegiance to symbols, we are failing to hold fast to the profession of our faith when we compromise the Word of God. We are charged with the responsibility of being prepared to answer and offer help to those who need it.

Often because we are ill-prepared, we exclude certain groups of people from the church. Christian leaders and counselors should be prepared to deal with pre- and post- abortion issues, the LGBTQIAPK community, and the lack of human interaction and economic deprivation that could result from artificial intelligence. Unfortunately, the church has in many cases been the most segregated institution. We cannot change our history, but we can change the future one life at a time simply with proper application of God's Word. We have erected fences where we should be building bridges. We have turned willfully and looked the other way when we should be studying our intersections in life. We are bound to collide at these intersections if we continue living recklessly. Before we can assist someone in tearing down walls erected by abuse, rejection, fear, and other tactics of the enemy, we must collectively and collaboratively tear down the walls which subdivide and categorize the church. Our lack of consensus is because we have not contended for the absolutism of God's word as the final authority. We have not agreed on its interpretation, because we would rather sooth and satisfy our own desires.

The church still has numerous things to address. First Peter 4:17

(KJV) says, "For the time is come that judgment must begin at the house of God: and if it first begins at us, what shall the end be of him that obey not the gospel of God?" Women are still not treated with respect in the church; and yet, the church expects to be heard in the fight against domestic violence, abortion, and gender inequality in the workplace. The misogynistic attitudes toward women who preach and teach the Word of God still thrives in conventions, fellowships, pulpits, and pews across America. Women are okay to write much of the Christian material used for Christian education. However, many of the churches have issues with women standing in a pulpit or teaching. What about xenophobia? How can we truly love God and hate His creation? Do we think God is unintelligent? I had a conversation with a mother who told me that her daughter wanted to spend time with her friend who happened to be Muslim. The mother refused to allow the children to hang out. Do we ever stop to think that our belief in Jesus as the Son of God should be able to stand in the presence of what we see as opposing thoughts and beliefs? Are we teaching our children to hold fast the profession of their faith without wavering even when they are in the presence of other people who may not believe what we believe? Many readers may disagree with me here. I understand that children have to be guided. However, we have to make sure that our guidance is not directed by prejudices, biases, and discrimination. Do we avoid people on our jobs and in communities who are from other countries? How dare we do so and think that God is pleased. Racism, classism, sexism, xenophobia, and misogyny are just a few of the things that separate us in the Body of Christ. How will we ever impact the world for Jesus without dealing with these issues which plague us? We tend to weaponize our argument concerning these issues to hurt and gain or maintain the upper hand. This is definitely what condemns but it definitely does not love.

As Americans continue to attribute future success to membership in a political party, we continue to miss the point. Are we so conservative that we exclude others and miss the opportunity to do the work of the kingdom? Are we so liberal that we exclude God for everyone else? How is it that we choose to be liberal in the love according to the world's way rather than in giving the love of God? Are we so independent that we no longer depend on the Holy Spirit to guide us? Are we so far to the right that we are self-righteous? Are we so conservative that we "save" the gospel for who we think is worthy enough? Second Chronicles 7:14 (KJV) says, "If my people, which are called by my name, shall humble themselves, and pray, and seek my face, and turn from their wicked ways; then will I hear from heaven, and will forgive their sin, and will heal their land."[387] As members of the Body of Christ, we cannot blame the world alone for its condition. We must be willing to conclude some things in order to begin the new things. We are ambassadors of the kingdom of God. Hence, we must tailor ministry to meet the needs of those who are in sin. We must take daily inventory of our own lives and hold fast the profession of our faith.[388] The writer of Hebrews warns us not to be of those who shrink back; instead, we are to have faith to the saving of souls.[389] Christians are facing and will continue facing difficult times. Persecution and suffering are eminent. However, we must maintain a steadfast perspective. The Apostle Paul says in 1 Corinthians 9:27 (KJV), "But I keep under my body, and bring it into subjection: lest that by any means, when I have preached to others, I myself should be a castaway."

Christians must never live as if having arrived at some utopia of perfection. Daily we should remember to give our total self to the service of the kingdom. We must remember Jesus' final words in John Chapter 16, "These things I have spoken unto you, that in me ye might have peace. In the world ye shall have tribulation: but be of good cheer; I have overcome the world."[390] Though, the problems we face be seemingly big, Jesus has conquered all. We must give Him glory as we lovingly lead others to Him with uncompromising compassion and without condemnation. There is nothing more rewarding than a personal relationship with the God of love. It is my prayer that readers know that Jesus' love has no boundaries. You have come to the completion of this book. My hope is that you will continue your journey with Christ. Romans 8:1 (KJV) says, "There is therefore now no condemnation to them which are in Christ Jesus, who walk not after the flesh, but after the Spirit. Always forward!

ENDNOTES

Chapter 1

1 Alex Murashko, "Excusive Rick Warren: 'Flat Out Wrong' That Muslims, Christians View God the Same," *The Christian Post*, March 2, 2012, https://www.christianpost.com/news/exclusive-rick-warren-flat-out-wrong-that-muslims-christians-view-god-the-same.html.

2 Jam. 4:17 (KJV).

3 Matt. 5:16 (KJV).

Chapter 2

4 Emrys Westacott, "Moral Relativism," *The Internet Encyclopedia of Philosophy*, https://www.iep.utm.edu/, (Accessed November 4, 2019).

5 Lucy Moll, "When Moral Relativism Comes to Counseling," June 5, 2019, https://www.lucyannmoll.com/when-moral-relativism-comes-to-counseling/.

6 Mark 8:22-26 (KJV).

7 Mark 8:24-26 (KJV).

8 Ibid.

9 Ibid.

10 Bible Study Tools, "Mark 8" Matthew Henry's Commentary on the Whole Bible Complete, https://www.biblestudytools.com/commentaries/matthew-henry-complete/mark/8.html (Accessed November 4, 2019).

11 Emrys Westacott, "Moral Relativism".

12 Ibid.

13 Emrys Westacott, "Moral Relativism."

14 Rob Gonda, "Adaptability Is Key to Survival in the Age of Digital Darwinism," *Forbes Magazine*, May 24, 2018, https://www.forbes.com/sites/forbestechcouncil/2018/05/24/adaptability-is-key-to-survival-in-the-age-of-digital-darwinism/.

15 "Moral Relativism," *The Stanford Encyclopedia of Philosophy*, April 20, 2015, https://plato.stanford.edu/entries/moralrelativism/ (Accessed November 9, 2019).

16 Mark M.H. Tan, "An Argument Against Ethical Subjectivism," *Think* 14, no. 41 (Autumn 2015): 69, https://doi.org/10.1017/S1477175615000299.

17 I John 3:4 (KJV).

18 "In act 1, scene 3, of Hamlet, what is Polonius's advice to Laertes?" *eNotes Editorial*, October 12, 2012, https://www.enotes.com/homework-help/in-act-1-scene-3-of-hamlet-what-is-polonius-s-366178.

19 Gregg Henriques, "The Elements of Ego Functioning: The six elements of ego functioning," *Psychology Today*, June 27, 2013, https://www.psychologytoday.com/us/blog/theory-knowledge/201306/the-elements-ego-functioning.

20 I Sam. 1:20 (KJV).

21 I Sam. 8:7 (KJV).

22 I Sam. 9:21 (KJV).

23 I Sam. 15:1-16 (KJV).

24 Ibid.

25 Esth. 9:24 (KJV).

26 Gen. 3:3 (KJV).

27 Courtney E. Ackerman, "What is Self-Concept Theory? A Psychologists Explains," *Positive Psychology*, August 11, 2019, https://positivepsychology.com/self-concept/.

28 Emma Law, "The Origin of the Saying 'When in Rome, Do as the Romans Do'," *Culture Trip*, February 22, 2018, https://theculturetrip.com/europe/italy/articles/the-origin-of-the-saying-when-in-rome-do-as-the-romans-do/.

29 Stephen Tillett, "Tolerance Isn't as Important as Inclusion," *Capital Gazette*, December 7, 2019, https://www.capitalgazette.com/opinion/columns/ace-column-tillett-20191207-gbewjojpkfbcbmt2sobhmy4so4-story.html.

30 Rom. 14:1-4 (KJV).

31 Eph. 4:2 (KJV).

32 Acts 17:22-31 (KJV).

33 Acts 17:23 (KJV).

34 Eph. 2:8 (KJV).

35 Ibid.

36 Rom. 6:1–2 (KJV).

37 Ibid.

38 Kyle Irwin and Brent Simpson, "Do Descriptive Norms Solve Social Dilemmas? Conformity and Contributions in Collective Action Groups," *Journal of Social Forces, 91,* no.3 (February 15, 2013): 1060.

39 Jam. 4:17 (KJV).

40 Robert Bean, *Sir William Osler Aphorisms from His Bedside Teachings and Writings*, (New York: Henry Schuman, Inc., 1950), 49.

41 Eugene Ahtirski, "Why Even Lawyers Hire Other Lawyers to Represent Their Interests in Legal Matters," *Legal Guide,* September 8, 2011, https://www.avvp.com/legal-guides/ugc/Abraham-lincoln-had-it-right---he-who-represents-himself-has-a-fool-for-a-client.

42 Psa. 41:1 (KJV).

43 Ibid.

44 WordNet 3.0. s.v. "idealistic.", https://www.thefreedictionary.com/idealistic (Accessed November 9, 2019).

45 Dictionary.com, s.v. "realist", (Random House, Inc. 2019), https://www.dictionary.com/browse/realist?s=t, (Accessed November 9, 2019).

46 David Olson, "Understanding the Idealistic Distortion Score," Prepare-Enrich, https://www.prepare-enrich.com/pe/pdf/counselor/HTSCV/idealistic_distortion.pdf (Accessed November 9, 2019).

47 Ibid.

48 Olson, "Idealistic Distortion Score".

49 Ibid.

50 Rom. 4:21 (KJV).

51 II Tim. 3:16 (KJV).

Chapter 3

52 R. Y. Langham, "What is Christian Counseling," *Therapy Tribe*, last modified April 19, 2019, https://www.therapytribe.com/therapy/christian-counseling/.

53 Ibid.

54 Jay Adams, "What Is Nouthetic Counseling," http://www.nouthetic.org/what-is-nouthetic-counseling (Accessed November 13, 2019).

55 Adams, "Nouthetic Counseling".

56 John 17:17 (KJV).

57 Gen. 2:21 (KJV).

58 Jer. 1:5 (KJV).

59 Isa. 64:8 (KJV).

60 Eph. 2:10 (KJV).

61 Rom. 5:8 (KJV).

62 Gal. 3:13-15 (KJV).

63 Psa. 1:1-3 (KJV).

64 Ibid.

65 I Cor. 1:25 (KJV).

66 Rom. 8:27 (KJV).

67 I Cor. 2: 6-14 (KJV).

68 Isa. 40:8 (KJV).

69 I Thess. 5:23 (KJV).

70 John 1:1 (KJV).

71 Mark 5:34 (KJV).

72 John 5:6 (KJV).

73 John 14:12-14 (KJV).

74 Heb. 13:8 (KJV).

75 I Pet. 4:8-9 (KJV).

76 Taruna Chhabra, "7 Types of Connective Tissue," *Sciencing*, https:// sciencing.com/7-types-connective-tissue-8768445.html (Accessed November 15, 2019).

77 *The Merriam-Webster.com Dictionary*, s.v. "blood," accessed December 27, 2019, https://www.merriam-webster.com/dictionary/blood.

78 Matt. 5:13 (KJV).

79 Jay Adams, "Empirical Evidence," October 25, 2017, http://www. nouthetic.org/blog/?p=3877 (Accessed November 20, 2019).

80 John 15:13-14 (KJV).

81 Ibid.

82 Eph. 3:18-19 (KJV).

83 Jer. 29:11 (KJV).

84 I Thess. 5:11 (KJV).

85 Eph. 4: 4-6 (KJV).

86 I John 4:20 (KJV).

87 Luke 18:27 (KJV).

88 Rom. 10:9-11 (KJV).

89 Matt. 28:19-20 (KJV).

90 Eph. 4:15 (KJV).

91 Gal. 4:16-18 (KJV).

92 Gen. 49:3-4 (KJV).

93 Ibid.

94 Charles Spurgeon, "Commentary on Genesis 49:4," *Spurgeon's Verse Expositions of the Bible 2011*, https://www.studylight.org/commentaries/ spe/genesis-49.html (Accessed November 20, 2019).

95 Rev. 3:15-17 (KJV).

96 John 14:15 (KJV).

97 Heb. 4:12 (KJV).

98 Heb. 9:22 (KJV).

Chapter 4

99 I Cor. 2:11 (KJV).

100 Matt. 10:16 (KJV).

101 Pamela Paul, "With God as My Shrink," *Psychology Today*, May 1, 2005, https://www.psychologytoday.com/us/articles/200505/god-my-shrink (Accessed November 26, 2019).

102 I John 4:1-6 (KJV).

103 Ibid.

104 Phil. 3:8-10 (KJV).

105 Ibid.

106 Acts 8:9-24 (KJV).

107 Acts 8:20-24 (KJV).

108 Ibid.

109 American Institute of Healthcare Professionals, "The Role of The Certified Christian Counselor," https://aihcp.net/the-role-of-the-certified-christian-counselor/ (Accessed November 26, 2019).

110 Jay E. Adams, *Helps for Counselors: A mini-manual for Christian Counseling* (Grand Rapides, MI: Baker Book House, 1979), 5.

111 Ab Abercrombie, "Counseling Unbelievers." *Biblical Counseling Institute*, (August 8, 2013), https://bcinstitute.com/counseling-unbelievers/ (Accessed November 13, 2019).

112 Acts 8:9-24 (KJV).

113 Luke 13:18-21 (KJV).

114 Ibid.

115 Ed Welch, "Biblical Counseling for Unbelievers," (April 22, 2015), https://www.ccef.org/biblical-counseling-unbelievers/ (Accessed November 12, 2019).

116 I Cor. 3:6 (KJV).

117 Isa. 30:18 (KJV).

118 II Tim. 1:9 (KJV).

119 Rom. 3:23-24 (KJV).

120 II Cor. 12:8-9 (KJV).

121 Dan. 3:16-28 (KJV).

Chapter 5

122 John 3:17 (KJV).

123 Ibid.

124 Rom. 6:23 (KJV).

125 John 10:10 (KJV).

126 Rom. 3:23 (KJV).

127 Ibid.

128 Ibid.

129 Ibid.

130 Ibid.

131 Ibid.

132 John 3:17 (KJV).

133 Phil. 1:7-8 (KJV).

134 Rom. 8:1 (KJV).

135 John 3:18 (KJV).

136 Rom. 7:19 (KJV).

137 Jam. 4:17 (KJV).

138 Goodreads, "Thomas Merton", https://www.goodreads.com/quotes/161733-our-job-is-to-love-others-without-stopping-to-inquire (Accessed December 1, 2019).

139 John 13:34 (KJV).

140 Jude 1:22-23 (KJV).

141 Phil. 3:9 (KJV).

142 Charles Spurgeon, Brainy Quotes, https://www.brainyquote.com/quotes/charles_spurgeon_181483 (Accessed December 1, 2019).

143 Edward T. Welch, "Is Biblical-Nouthetic Counseling Legalistic? Reexamination of a Biblical Theme," *Journal of Biblical Counseling* 11, no.1 (1992): 4.

144 Ibid.

145 Welch, "Biblical Theme", 4.

146 II Tim. 4:2 (KJV).

147 Ibid.

148 Romans 5:8 (KJV).

149 Jer. 31:3 (KJV).

150 Heb. 12:6-7 (KJV).

151 Ibid.

152 Joseph, "Unconditional Positive Regard."

153 Kristin Kansiewicz, "Increasing Accessibility: When Proximity Works," Church Therapy Associates, September 30, 2018, https://www.churchtherapy.com/2018/09/30/increasing-accessibility-when-proximity-works, (Accessed November 21, 2019).

154 Les Parrott and Leslie Parrott, The Complete Guide to Marriage Mentoring: Connecting Couples to Build Better Marriages, (Grand Rapids: Zondervan, 2005), 48.

155 Courtney E. Ackerman, "What is Unconditional Positive Regard in Psychology," Positive Psychology, October 17, 2019, https://positvepsychology.com/unconditional-positve-regard/, (Accessed November 20, 2019.

156 Ackerman, "Regard in Psychology".

157 Phil. 2:3-5 (KJV).

158 Ibid.

159 Lam. 3:22 (KJV).

160 Barbara McMahon, "Unconditional Positive Regard in Parenting," February 16, 2013, https://www.barbaramcmahon.org, (Accessed November 20, 2019).

161 Ackerman, "Regard in Psychology".

162 I Pet. 4:8 (KJV).

163 Rev. 12:11 (KJV).

164 II Cor. 5:21 (KJV).

165 Emma Bedford, "Valentine's Day Spending in the United States from 2004 to 2019 (in billion U.S. dollars)," Statista, August 20, 2019, https://www.statista.com/statistics/673236/us-valentine-s-day-spending/, (Accessed November 28, 2019).

166 Jay Lowder, "The Universal Language of Love," Charisma Magazine, https://www.charismamag.com/life/relationships/19773-the-universal-language-of-love, (Accessed November 22, 2019).

167 Joaquin Selva, "Abraham Maslow, His Theory & Contribution to Psychology" *Positive Psychology,* November 11, 2019, https://positivepsychology.com/abraham-maslow/, (Accessed November 29, 2019).

168 Ibid.

169 I John 4:7-10 (KJV).

170 Maria Baghramian and J. Adam Carter, "Relativism", *The Stanford Encyclopedia of Philosophy* (Winter 2019 Edition), Edward N. Zalta ed., https://plato.stanford.edu/archives/win2019/entries/relativism, (Accessed December 28, 2019).

171 Exo. 20:3 (KJV).

172 Rom. 7:19 (KJV).

173 Deut. 6:4-5 (KJV).

174 Eph. 4:5-6 (KJV).

175 Rom. 8:39 (KJV).

176 John 14:20 (KJV).

177 Nikolaj Jang Lee Linding Pedersen and Cory Wright, "Pluralist Theories of Truth", *The Stanford Encyclopedia of Philosophy*, Winter 2018, Edward N. Zalta ed., https://plato.stanford.edu/archives/win2018/entries/truth-pluralist/, (Accessed December 15, 2019).

178 Matt. 6:24 (KJV).

179 II Cor. 6:14 (KJV).

180 Mark 10:8 (KJV).

181 Eph. 2:19-20 (KJV).

182 Ibid.

183 Heb. 10:25 (KJV).

184 I Cor. 1:10 (KJV).

185 I Tim. 4:12 (KJV).

186 Luke 13:18-21 (KJV).

Chapter 6

187 Jeffrey Jones, "U.S. Church Membership Down Sharply in Past Two Decades," *Gallup Poll*, April 18, 2019, https://news.gallup.com/poll/248837/church-membership-down-sharply-past-two-decades.aspx, (Accessed December 1, 2019).

188 Ibid.

189 Ibid.

190 Jones, "U.S. Church Membership".

191 Ibid.

192 Jamie Manson, "As U.S. 'Nones' Increase, We Must Start Asking Different Questions," *National Catholic Reporter*, October 19, 2019, https://www.ncronline.org/news/opinion/grace-margins/us-nones-increase-we-must-start-asking-different-questions, (Accessed December 19, 2019).

193 II Tim. 2:15 (KJV).

194 Luke 14:23 (KJV).

195 John 14:12-14 (KJV).

196 II Tim. 1:9 (KJV).

197 Col. 4:6 (KJV).

198 Jer. 33:3 (KJV).

199 Ibid.

200 Exo. 3:14 (KJV).

201 Rom. 1:7 (KJV).

202 Zane Hodges, "Romans 1: A Concise Commentary," *Grace in Focus*, November/December 2019, 13-20.

203 Rom. 1:18 (KJV).

204 Rom. 1:22 (KJV).

205 Rom. 1:28-32 (KJV).

206 Ibid.

207 II Tim. 1:16 (KJV).

208 II Tim 1:8-18 (KJV).

209 Ibid.

210 II Tim. 2:16 (KJV).

211 II Tim. 3:1-5 (KJV).

212 II Tim. 3:8 (KJV).

213 II Tim. 4:2 (KJV).

214 Ibid.

215 John 3:2 (KJV).

216 John 3:4 (KJV).

217 Luke 17:21 (KJV).

218 Rom. 6:1 (KJV).

219 David Powlison, "How Does Sanctification Work (Part 3)", *The Journal of Biblical Counseling* 31, no. 1(2017): 9-32.

220 Powlison, "Sanctification Work", 11.

221 Ibid.

222 Rom. 12:1 (KJV).

223 Rom. 10:10 (KJV).

224 Rom. 1:17b (KJV).

225 Rom. 5:1 (KJV).

226 Hab. 2:4 (KJV).

227 Gen. 15:6 (KJV).

228 Rom. 4:3 (KJV).

229 Phil. 3:9 (KJV).

230 Gal. 3:29 (KJV).

231 Rom. 10:4 (KJV).

232 Matthew 6:8 (KJV).

233 John 19:30 (KJV).

Chapter 7

234 Heb. 13:8 (KJV).

235 Psalm 118:89 (KJV).

236 Jer. 1:12 (KJV).

237 Eccl. 1:9 (KJV).

238 I Cor. 6:19 (KJV).

239 Eph. 3:16-18 (KJV).

240 II Sam. 5:17-25 (KJV).

241 Prov. 3:5-6 (KJV).

242 II Sam. 12:19-20 (KJV).

243 Matt 5:18 (KJV).

244 John Turner, "Neutering God," *Anxious Bench*, May 1, 2013, https://www.patheos.com/blogs/anxiousbench/2013/05/neutering-god/,.

245 Father Mark Hodges, "U.S. Episcopal Diocese Votes to Stop Using Masculine Pronouns for God," *LifeNews*, February 1, 2018, https://www.

lifenews.com/news/u.s.-episcopal-dioces-votes-to-stop-using-masculine-pronouns-for-God.

246 Wayne Grudem and Jerry Thacker, *Why Is My Choice of a Bible Translation So Important?* (Louisville, KY: Council on Biblical Manhood and Womanhood, 2005).

247 Eric Andersen, "Neutering the Bible," *Steadfast Lutherans*, March 20, 2013, https://steadfastlutherans.org/2013/03/neutering-the-bible/.

248 Ibid.

249 Gen 17:1 (KJV).

250 Ibid.

251 Num. 27:1-11 (KJV).

252 John 3:16 (KJV).

253 Isa. 9:6 (KJV).

254 Heb. 10:23 (KJV).

Chapter 8

255 Adam Liptak, "Supreme Court Ruling Makes Same-Sex Marriage a Right Nationwide," *New York Times*, June 26, 2015, https://www.nytimes.com/2015/06/27/us/supreme-court-same-sex-marriage.html, (Accessed December 3, 2019).

256 The White House Office of the Press Secretary, "FACT SHEET: Obama Administration's Record and the LGBT Community", June 9, 2016, https://obamawhitehouse.archives.gov/the-press-office/2016/06/09/fact-sheet-obama-administrations-record-and-lgbt-community, (Accessed December 3, 2019).

257 Amy Sutherland, "LGBTQIAPK: Let's Unpack the Acronym," *Harlot*, March 29, 2018, https:www.google.com/amp/s/ https://www.callmeharlot.com/all-learning-content/lgbtqiapk-lets-unpack-the-acronym, (Accessed August 24, 2019).

258 Jer. 17:9 (KJV).

259 Rom. 7:18 (KJV).

260 Noah Nevils, "What Are the Four Types of Love in the Bible," *Bible Reasons*, October 16, 2019, https://biblereasons.com/what-are-the-4-types-of-love-in-the-bible/.

261 Isa. 49:15 (KJV).)

262 Phil. 2:3 (KJV).

263 Nevils, "Love in the Bible."

264 Gen. 4:1-16 (KJV).

265 Nevils, "Love in the Bible."

266 Nevils, "Love in the Bible."

267 Rom. 1:26 (KJV).

268 II Tim. 3:16 (KJV).

269 Rom. 12:1 (KJV).

270 Rom. 12:2 (KJV).

271 Ibid.

272 Psa. 23:5 (KJV).

273 John 15 (KJV).

274 Psa. 51:5 (KJV).

275 Tim Stafford, "Getting Serious About Lust in an Age of Smirks," *The Journal of the Bible* 13, no. 13, Spring 1995, 4.

276 Col. 3:1-5 (KJV).

277 Rodney M. Perry, "Obergefell v. Hodges: Same-Sex Marriage Legalized*",* *Congressional Research Service*, August 7, 2015, https://fas.org/sgp/crs/misc/R44143.pdf.

278 Gen. 2:22-23 (KJV).

279 Ibid.

280 Matt. 26:28 (KJV).

281 Matt 1:1-17 (KJV).

282 John 15:1-8 (KJV).

283 Ibid.

284 Gen. 1:27-28 (KJV) emphasis mine.

285 Ibid.

286 John 15:4 (KJV).

287 Matt.19:3-5 (KJV).

288 Michael D. Waggoner, "When the Court Took on Prayer and the Bible in Public Schools", *Religion and Politics*, June 25, 2012, https://religionandpolitics.org/2012/06/25/when-the-court-took-on-prayer-the-bible-and-public-schools/, (Accessed December 12,2019).

289 Saul McLeod, "Erik Erikson's Stages of Psychosocial Development," *Simply Psychology*, https://www.simplypsychology.org/simplypsychology.org-Erik-Erikson.pdf, (Accessed December 12, 2019).

290 Ibid.

291 Ibid.

292 Ibid.

293 I Sam. 2:22 (KJV).

294 I Sam. 4:4 (KJV).

295 I Sam. 4:19-21 (KJV).

296 Rom. 1:27 (KJV).

297 Eph. 2:8-10 (KJV).

298 I Cor. 6:19 (KJV).

299 Jeff Buchanan, "The New Sexual Identity Crisis," *The Gospel Coalition*, July 10, 2012, https://www.thegospelcoalition.org/article/the-new-sexual-identity-crisis-2/.

300 Eph. 2:14 (KJV).

301 I Sam. 2:2 (KJV).

302 John 8:12 (KJV).

303 John 10:10 (KJV).

304 John 1:1-3 (KJV).

305 John 15:7 (KJV).

306 Exo. 32:1 (KJV).

307 Isa. 45:23 (KJV).

308 "Publishing Information." In the Oxford Dictionary of Proverbs, Oxford University Press, 2008. https://www.oxfordreference.com/view/10.1093/acref/9780199539536.001.0001/acref-9780199539536-div1-1429.

309 Heb. 12:28 (KJV).

310 Phil. 2:10-11 (KJV).

311 Isa. 53:5 (KJV).

Chapter 9

312 Lexico Powered by Oxford, s.v. "abortion," accessed December 12, 2019, https://www.lexico.com/definition/abortion.

313 Planned Parenthood, "What Facts About Abortion Do I Need to Know," https://www.plannedparenthood.org/learn/abortion/considering-abortion/what-facts-about-abortion-d-i-need-know, (Accessed December 16, 2019).

314 Michele Ye Hee Lee, "The Stale Claim That 'one in three' Women Will Have an Abortion by Age 45", *The Washington Post*, September 30, 2015, https://www.washingtonpost.com/news/fact-checker/wp/2015/09/30/the-stale-claim-that-one-in-three-women-will-have-an-abortion-by-age-45/?arc404=true.

315 Rachel Jones and Jenna Jerman, "Abortion Incidence and Service Availability In the United States, 2011," *Perspectives on Sexual and Reproductive Health, Guttmacher Institute*, 46, no. 1, (March 2014), https://www.guttmacher.org/sites/default/files/pdfs/journals/psrh.46e0414.pdf.

316 Planned Parenthood, "What Facts About Abortion".

317 Susan A. Cohen, "Facts and Consequences: Legality, Incidence and Safety of Abortion Worldwide," *Guttmacher Institute* 12, no. 4, (November 9, 2009), https://www.guttmacher.org/gpr/2009/11/facts-and-consequences-legality-incidence-and-safety-abortion-worldwide.

318 Tara C. Jatlaoui et al., "Abortion Surveillance — United States, 2016," *Morbidity and Mortality Weekly Report Surveillance Summary 2019*, 68, no. 11 (November 29, 2019), pg. 1–41, http://dx.doi.org/10.15585/mmwr.ss6811a1external icon.

319 Jamie Ducharme, "U. S. Birth Rates Hit a Record Low in 2018," *Time Health*, Summer 2019: 9.

320 Psa. 139:13 (KJV).

321 Jer. 29:11 (KJV).

322 John 10:10 (KJV).

323 Roe v. Wade, Oyez, US 410,113, https://www.oyez.org/cases/1971/70-18, (Accessed December 16, 2019).

324 Ibid.

325 Isa. 44:24 (KJV).

326 Gal. 1:15 (KJV).

327 John 14:6 (KJV).

328 Allison Cavanaugh, "The Term 'Pro-Life' Should Be Changed To 'Pro-Birth,' And Here's Why," *The Odyssey Online*, May 29, 2019, https://www.theodysseyonline.com/new-alabama-abortion-law, (Accessed December 5, 2019).

329 "Voting Rights for African Americans," Library of Congress, https://www.loc.gov/teachers/classroommaterials/presentationsandactivities/presentations/elections/voting-rights-african-americans.html, (Accessed December 19, 2019).

330 Mic. 6:8 (KJV).

331 Isa. 1:17 (KJV).

332 Abby Attia, "7 Reasons Why Planned Parenthood Should Not Get Government Money," *My Heritage*, https://www.myheritage.org/news/7-reasons-why-planned-parenthood-should-not-get-government-money/, (Accessed December 19, 2019).

333 Isa. 49:15 (KJV).

334 Louisiana Right to Life, https://prolifelouisiana.or/louisian-abortion-statistics/, (Accessed July 16, 2020).

335 Ibid.

336 Ibid.

337 Ibid.

338 Heb. 13:3 (KJV).

339 Matt. 25:36 (KJV).

340 Prov. 22:6 (KJV).

341 Gal. 5:9 (KJV).

342 II Chron. 7:14 (KJV).

343 Pat Layton, "Healing the Guilt and Pain of Abortion," *LifeWay*, October 30, 2018, https://www.lifeway.com/en/articles/homelife-women-healing-the-guilt-and-pain-of-abortion.

344 Care Net, "Study of Women Who Have Had an Abortion and Their Views on Church," *LifeWay Research*, http://lifewayresearch.com/wp-content/uploads/2015/11/Care-Net-Final-Presentation-Report-Revised.pdf, (Accessed December 19, 2019).

345 Ibid.

346 Ibid.

347 Ibid.

348 Ibid.

349 Christine Hoover, "In Her Shoes: One Woman's Testimony about Abortion and God's Grace," *The Journal of Biblical Counseling* 29, no. 2, (2015): 36-44.

350 David Powlison, "A Personal Liturgy of Confession", *The Journal of Biblical Counseling* 29, no. 2, (2015): 45-52.

Chapter 10

351 Gen. 38:9-10 (KJV).

352 Ibid.

353 Patrick Fagan, "The Effects of Pornography on Individuals, Marriage, Family, and Community," *Family Research Council,* March 2011, https://downloads.frc.org/EF/EF11C36.pdf, (Accessed December 19, 2019).

354 Jennifer A. Johnson, Matthew B. Ezzell, Ana J. Bridges, and Chyng F. Sun, "Pornography and Heterosexual Women's Intimate Experiences

with a Partner," *Journal of Women's Health 28,*, no. 9, (April 18, 2019): 1254-1265, http://doi.org/10.1089/jwh.2018.7006.

355 Gen. 2:18 (KJV).

356 Centers for Disease Control, "Human Papillomavirus (HPV)", https://www.cdc.gov/hpv/parents/about-hpv.html, (Accessed December 19, 2019).

357 Sanjay Mehta, "Sildenafil for Pulmonary Arterial Hypertension," *Chest Journal* 123, no. 4, (April 2003): 989–992, https://doi.org/10.1378/chest.123.4.989.

358 Ibid.

Chapter 11

359 Heb. 3:12 (KJV).

360 Jamie Manson, "As U.S. 'Nones' Increase, We Must Start Asking Different Questions," *National Catholic Reporter*, October 19, 2019, https://www.ncronline.org/news/opinion/grace-margins/us-nones-increase-we-must-start-asking-different-questions.

361 Thom Schultz, "The Rise of the Dones: The 'Done With Church' Population," *Church Leaders*, February 23, 2018, https://churchleaders.com/outreach-missions/outreach-missions-articles/177144-thom-schultz-rise-of-the-done-with-church-population.html.

362 John 14:12-14 (KJV).

363 Mark 8:36 (KJV).

364 II Tim. 1:7 (KJV).

365 B. J. Copeland, "Artificial Intelligence," *Encyclopedia Britannica*, November 19, 2019, https://www.britannica.com/technology/artificial-intelligence.

366 "Emotional Intelligence," *Psychology Today*, https://www.psychologytoday.com/us/basics/emotional-intelligence (Accessed December 15, 2019).

367 Alex Hern, "What is the Turing Test? And are We All Doomed Now," *The Guardian*, June 9, 2014, https://www.theguardian.com/technology/2014/jun/09/what-is-the-alan-turing-test, (Accessed December 19, 2019).

368 Sean Hays, "Transhumanism: Social and Philosophical Movement," *Encyclopedia Britannica*, June 12, 2018, https://www.britannica.com/topic/transhumanism.

369 Victoria Lorrimer, "Artificial Intelligence and Apocalypticism," *The Journal of Religion and Science* 54, no.1, (March, 2019): 191-206, https://doi.org/10.1111/zygo.12481.

370 Ibid.

371 Bill Joy, "Why the Future Doesn't Need Us," *Wired*, April 1, 2000, https://www.wired.com/2000/04/joy-2/.

372 Noreen Herzfeld, "Creating in Our Own Image: Artificial Intelligence and the Image of God," *Journal of Religion and Science* 37, no. 2, (June 2002): 304.

373 Ibid, 306.

374 Ibid.

375 II Cor. 12:9-11 (KJV).

376 Levchuk, "AI vs. God".

377 Matt, 6:33 (KJV).

378 Exo. 32:4-5 (KJV).

379 Ibid.

380 William Hill, Quotes and Thoughts, https://thoughtsfortoday2016.wordpress.com/, (Accessed December 12, 2019).

381 Ibid.

382 Gen. 4:6 (KJV).

Chapter 12

383 Gal. 4:16 (KJV).

384 Eph. 4:15 (KJV).

385 Psa. 33:12 (KJV).

386 Prov. 14:34 (KJV).

387 II Chron. 7:14 (KJV).

388 Heb. 10:23 (KJV).

389 Heb. 10:39 (KJV).

390 John 16:33 (KJV).